# CROSS & CROZIER

## The History of the Diocese of Saint Augustine

Written By
Charles Gallagher, Ph.D.

Edited By
Kathleen Bagg-Morgan

ÉDITIONS
DU SIGNE

Author: Charles Gallagher, Ph.D.

Editor:   Kathleen Bagg-Morgan
          Director of Communications, Diocese of Saint Augustine, Fla.

Cover photos:   "The Great Cross," a 208 foot stainless steel cross, located on the grounds of
                Mission Nombre de Dios in St. Augustine.

                A detail of an oil painting of "The First Mass" that hung in the Cathedral of
                St. Augustine prior to the 1887 fire. Father Francisco Lopez de Mendoza
                Grajales celebrated a Mass of Thanksgiving on Sept. 8, 1565, the same day the
                City of St. Augustine was founded.

Cover design: Patrick McKinney, Dalton Agency, Jacksonville, Fla.

Cover photos: Frantisek Zvardon

Publisher: Editions du Signe - B.P.94- 67038 Strasbourg - France

Publishing Director: Christian Riehl

Design and Layout:  Patrick McKinney, Dalton Agency, Jacksonville, Florida

Director of Publication:  Dr. Claude-Bernard Costecalde
Printed in France by PPO Graphic, 93500 Pantin

# Forward

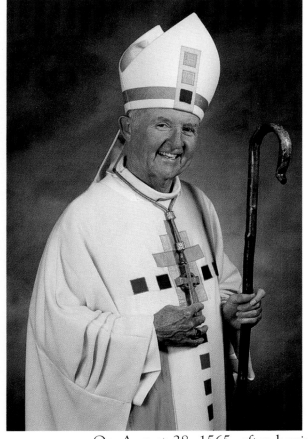

PEACE IN CHRIST

Dear Friends in Christ:

It was just five years ago that the Diocese of Saint Augustine celebrated its 125th Anniversary of its founding. Today, on the occasion of the Great Jubilee Year 2000, we celebrate a "Year of the Lord's Favor." However, before we usher in the Third Millennium, it is appropriate to reflect on the struggles and achievements of those who brought the Catholic Faith to the "New World" 435 years ago.

On August 28, 1565, after having sailed up the coast of present-day Florida, the Menendez expedition discovered land west of Anastasia Island. They named the spot St. Augustine in honor of the saint on whose feast day they sighted land. It is here that our story begins.

It is a story that takes place 55 years before the landing of the Puritan Pilgrims at Plymouth Rock, 40 years before the British settled the colony of Jamestown, and more than 210 years before the American Revolution. It is a story filled with well-known names of men and women, clergy and religious, who shaped the Catholic history of "La Florida."

Our story comes vividly to life in the text and colorful illustrations of *Cross & Crozier: The History of the Diocese of Saint Augustine*. Written by Charles Gallagher, Ph.D., *Cross & Crozier* provides a popular treatment of the history of the Mother Diocese of Florida. It records how Catholics struggled for their faith, endured many hardships and witnessed effectively to gospel values.

My hope is that this book, as it commemorates the years of change, struggle and triumph for the people of the Diocese of Saint Augustine, will find a prominent place in our homes, our parishes and our schools.

While *Cross & Crozier* provides us with a rich resource for remembering our past, we must also look with hope to our future and realize that there are new challenges that we will be called upon to face with courage and ever deepening faith in the Lord Jesus.

With a blessing, I am

Sincerely Yours in Christ,

+ John J. Snyder

Bishop of Saint Augustine

# TABLE OF CONTENTS

*Cross & Crozier: The History of the Diocese of Saint Augustine*

# The Discoverers

## 1 5 1 3 - 1 5 6 5

*"Almighty and Eternal Lord God, Who by thy Sacred Word has created heaven, earth, and sea, blessed and glorified be thy Name and praised be Thy Majesty, and grant that through Thy humble servant, Thy Sacred Name may be known and preached in this other part of the world. Amen."*

— Attributed to Christopher Columbus, upon whose second voyage in 1494 Juan Ponce de Leon was a royal officer.

LEFT: A map of *Florida and the Caribbean, circa 1500s.*

In the distance, a faint silhouette of rising land met the naked eye. The men aboard three small ships under the command of Juan Ponce de León, the Spanish governor of Puerto Rico, scrambled from below decks to cast their first glance at what was to become their "New World." In 1513, this new land was thought to be the "Island of Bimini," a world which had been surrendered to the ages and one which extended abundant opportunities for the mining of gold, the attainment of political glory for the kingdom of Spain, and the worldly extension of the celestial kingdom of God. But Juan Ponce, reared on the Iberian Peninsula of Spain, had not discovered a new island paradise at all, he and his band of seafaring men had discovered a new peninsula, the southernmost point of what is now the United States of America.

Upon first sight of land, Juan Ponce knelt down and uttered the words, "Thanks be to thee, O Lord, Who has permitted me to see something new." These few words, as they echoed across the waves, were the first Christian intonations to be heard within the shores of what is now the United States. Juan Ponce's words became the watchwords for future centuries of Christian progress within this pristine and foreign domain. Indeed, the land was "something new."

It was Eastertide, 1513, and Roman Catholicism, tied so closely to the state in 16th century Spain, was about to make contact with the ancient ground which Juan Ponce would name *Pasqua florida* - Easter of the flowers. Later, this land would come to be known simply as "La Florida." The sands of Florida which Juan Ponce and his men first set to the heels of their boots were located just south of modern day

Cape Canaveral, a fitting premonition for the future space explorations of "New Worlds" which later generations would probe from the same spot. One wonders what thoughts raced through the minds of these new European voyagers as they gazed upon the white beaches where palmetto and pine met sand and sea. Lonely, desolate, but ever inspiring were these shores. Over the next 50 years, other Spanish explorers would come under the same spell of "La Florida's" dazzling white coastal lands.

In 1517, while the voyage of Francisco Hernandez de Córdova was making a return run from the Bahamas to Cuba, his ship was blown off course and took refuge in a harbor on Florida's west coast. It is surmised that the ship's chaplain, Father Alonzo González, became the first ordained Roman Catholic priest to spy the waters of Spanish Florida.

In 1521, Juan Ponce returned. This time he brought with him diocesan priests to minister to his own people, and missionaries of religious orders to evangelize the natives, whom the Spanish had mistakenly referred to since the sailing of Christopher Columbus as "Indians." These Native Americans were descendants of Asian peoples who had crossed the Bering Straits during the last 70,000 years of the Ice Age. The "land bridge" which provided passage for animals and humans between Asia and North America was subsequently covered by melting glaciers and rising seas. The new natives were in the Americas to stay. Yet, the 16th century contact with Europeans would throw their age-old culture and living space into perennial turmoil. When Juan Ponce returned to Florida in 1521, the Native Americans lined the shore to meet him. But the greeting was far from cordial. "Suspicion and hostility," the historian Robert Wooster has remarked, "stemming from technological and cultural differences, as well as mutual feelings of superiority, have permeated relations between Indians and non-Indians in North America."

While the precise location of the 1521 landing is not known, the landing does, for the first time, authenticate the first appearance of Catholic priests within the boundaries of present-day United States. The foreign dress, tongue, and mystical religion of the discoverers both threatened and infuriated the Native Americans, who attacked the landing party and wounded Juan Ponce with an expertly placed arrow through his thigh. Juan Ponce died in Cuba of the fatal wounds received on Florida's shores. The legacy of Juan Ponce was carried forward 18 years later when the intrepid 38-year-old Hernando de Soto landed just south of Tampa Bay, near present-day

ABOVE: *16th-century Timucua Indians encounter Spanish explorers.*

Bradenton on May 25, 1539. With him were eight secular priests and four Dominican friars. The Dominicans, otherwise known as the Order of Preachers, were established by Saint Dominic in 1216. As missionaries, their calling was to "proclaim the Word of God by preaching, teaching, and example," while holding to a communal way of life.

Wandering for months along the Gulf of Mexico toward Tallahassee, De Soto and his Dominican companions slashed through thick growth and battled thirst, disease, and Native-American hostility. Proceeding toward Alabama, De Soto and his troops brutally killed more than 2,000 Native Americans; De Soto lost only 18 men. The Spaniard, who was once described by a fellow Catholic as "preeminent in the points of cruelty," wandered northward until he met his own demise of malarial fever in 1542. Over the course of the expedition, De Soto's 12 accompanying priests also met their deaths. While the laws of Christian charity became obscured by De Soto's brutal drive toward conquest, eventually one missionary "sought to win the natives by kindness."

In 1549, Dominican Father Louis Cáncer de Barbastro set sail from Havana, Cuba for the Florida coast. Cancer was a seasoned Spaniard from the rugged region around Saragossa in northern Spain. After joining the Dominicans at the famed seminary in Salamanca, he

volunteered for the American missions and spent the greater portion of his life ministering to warring tribes in Guatemala. To his Guatemalan mission he brought an infinite trust in peaceful negotiation founded in Christlike charity and meekness. Father Cáncer's peaceful teaching methods met with great success in Central America, but when he applied them to his Floridian flock, he met with disaster. As his unarmed boat, the *Santa María de la Encina* sailed into Tampa Bay on June 25, 1549, only his God knew what was in store.

Sailing into the bay, Father Cáncer and his companions saw a group of heavily armed Native Americans gathered on shore. "For the love of God!," Father Gregorio de Beteta urged his leader, "Do not land!" Father Beteta knew that the Native Americans of Tampa Bay were surely enraged and recalled vividly the destructive legacy of De Soto and his conquistadors. Fearless, Father Cáncer had faith that his Lord would spare him from harm. If he could only have the opportunity to touch the lives of these men and women who waited for him on shore, he could impress them with his genuine good will and his peaceful soul. His plan was to have Father Gregorio navigate one of the ship's small lifeboats toward the shore and drop him off on the beach. As he approached the beach in his small craft, he said a prayer,

slipped over the side of his small boat, and made for land. As his body broke through the waves, he carried his wooden crucifix above his head. "Lift high the cross," Saint Paul wrote to the Christians at Corinth, and this Father Cáncer did. When he reached the shore he knelt and kissed Florida soil. Immediately, a young native broke from the group and dashed toward the priest.

Father Cáncer must have thought his prayers were answered when he received a warm and encouraging embrace from the young man. Buoyed by the reception, Father Cáncer accompanied his host to the waiting group of men. Now, the group raised their clubs against the priest and beat him mercilessly. For the first time, the blood of a man raised to Holy Priesthood had mixed with the Florida sands. In Rome, Father Louis Cáncer de Barbastro's violent death came as a complete shock. He is acknowledged as the first priest to perish on present-day American soil as a martyr for the Catholic Faith. Even more, Father Cáncer's heroic and bloody sacrifice failed to dissuade other Spanish Catholics from colonizing the Florida coasts.

"We endeavor, in every manner and by all means within our power to spread the Faith of Christ, our Redeemer, so that all nations may come to the knowledge of God and save their souls," Archbishop Alfonso de Montufar wrote to King Charles V of Spain in 1555. The archbishop was concerned that Florida exploration would not continue and therefore bypass a new chance for spreading the Faith. By 1558, King Philip II, who succeeded Charles in 1557, recognized that Florida once again had to be colonized and evangelized for the Empire.

UPPER RIGHT: *Philip II, King of Spain from 1558-1603.*

ABOVE: *A 16th-century navigational chart.*

By 1559, a conglomeration of Christian missionaries and Spanish legionnaires were being fitted out for another foray into the wilds of the Florida peninsula. This time, Philip II chose Don Tristán De Luna y Arellano, a nobleman of high birth who happened to be a relative of the viceroy of New Spain, to head-up the new mission. On May 12, 1559, De Luna was named "Illustrious Governor and General of La Florida."

On June 11, 1559, De Luna set out from Vera Cruz, Mexico and headed his 13 ships toward the safe harbors along Florida's coast. On August 14, the eve of the Feast of the Assumption, De Luna landed at Pensacola Bay. Then, anticipating Florida as the "fun capital" of the United States by 400 years, De Luna authorized that the expedition partake in a week-long festival of games. The carefree sporting events included horse races on the beach, boat races on the bay, and the festive consumption of many provisions on board ship. Soon, the festive atmosphere dissipated as De Luna's 500 soldiers, 1,000 colonists, and 240 horses set out to explore new ground and search for friendly natives.

One group of scouts went overland to chart the territory. The second group was sent in small boats up the narrow rivers of the region. Six

ABOVE LEFT: *Charles V, King of Spain from 1519 to 1558.*

BELOW: *Hernando De Soto's march through Florida in 1540 as illustrated in A History of Florida by Caroline Mays Brevard, 1904.*

ABOVE: *The area of six rivers in Florida (now known as Ft. Caroline) that the French discovered in 1564. Artist: Charles de la Roncière.*

BELOW: *Spanish soldiers as depicted robbing a Native American temple during the 16th century.*

Dominicans — Fathers Pedro de Feria, Domingo de la Annunción, Domingo de Salazar, Juan Mazuelas, Diego de San Domingo, and the brave Brother Bartolomé Matéos, accompanied the search parties as they probed Florida's thickly wooded interior. Soon, supplies ran low and both parties began to face starvation in the tropical jungles of the interior. Meanwhile, back in Pensacola Bay, a hurricane bore down on De Luna and his ships. The winds smashed the ships onto the shore and bolts of lightning illuminated the skies in golden flashes. The settlers blazed a trail into the brush and weathered the storm. When the reconnaissance groups returned to their home base, morale was so low that the ministry of the Dominicans was given over to promoting peace within the beleaguered camp. By 1561, De Luna had decided that his missionary venture had failed miserably. Death, destruction, and dissension were all that accompanied him on his voyage.

There were no precious metals, no prized gems, and not one Native American convert to send back to the court of Philip II at the magnificent Escorial near Madrid. Regardless of the failed prior attempts at colonization, Spain decided to try one last time to permanently settle "La Florida." This time, Philip II enlisted the aid of an undaunted commercial adventurer. Spurred by the prospect of still undiscovered wealth, another exploration was undertaken in 1565. This time, the labors of discovery would produce a permanent and solid monument to Spanish ingenuity.

# The Settlers

## 1 5 6 5 - 1 7 6 3

*"As I went ashore the evening before, I took the Cross and went to meet Menéndez, singing the hymn Te Deum Laudamus. The Admiral, followed by all who accompanied him, marched up to the Cross, knelt, and kissed it. A large number of Indians watched these proceedings and imitated all they saw done."*

— Father Francisco López de Mendoza Grajales, one of four diocesan priests accompanied the Menéndez expedition, described the landing on the shores of St. Augustine in his daily journal.

ABOVE: *The Spanish Coat of Arms that is located over the entrance to Fort Marion.*

LEFT: *A Charles de la Ronciere painting depicting French settlers and Native Americans.*

The future of Florida, the name by which the entire United States was known in 1565, laid in the hands of one intrepid Spanish military commander. Pedro Menéndez de Avilés was born on February 15, 1519 and hailed from the town of Aviles, a seaport in the northwest of Spain on the Bay of Biscay. Great achievements were expected from this new scion of noble birth. Pedro, whose father was a distinguished soldier for the Spanish crown, had 20 brothers and sisters by the time of his father's death in 1532. At age 14, Menéndez ran away from his crowded home to make his way in the world. By age 15, it is recorded, the young Menéndez was in command of his own corsair. Menéndez spent his teen years preying upon the commerce and harrying the coasts of unfriendly nations. Moreover, Menéndez had been commissioned and authorized by his government to undertake this perilous lifestyle.

The classroom of Pedro's youth was the sea, and his only tests were those of courage. By 1549, Menéndez had compiled an enviable record as a Spanish buccaneer. The key to his fame was the successful capture of the famous French marauder, Jean Alfonse. In 1554, Menéndez was named "Captain General of the Fleets of the Indies," and given a powerful position on the Spanish Board of Trade.

The fame of Menéndez, by now, had reached the ears of King Philip II of Spain and Francis Borgia, Father General of the newly formed Society of Jesus, commonly known as the Jesuits. Of course it helped his cause that Borgia, who would later be made a saint, was also a cousin of Menéndez. Regardless, King Philip II was once again looking to exploit Florida for undiscovered riches, and Borgia, as well, saw an opportunity for his "legions" of Jesuits to convert native inhabitants to the Cross. In 1564, Menéndez approached King Philip with the request that he outfit one more expedition to Florida. This time, Menéndez sought to use his position on the Board of Trade to control the economic markets in the region and become the primary profit-maker in the new territory. One noted historian has pointed out that Pedro Menéndez hoped to become "Florida's first great land developer, industrialist and agribusinessman." His wishes were also prompted by the hope that he might conduct a search of the region for his seagoing son, Don Juan Menéndez, who had been lost at sea on a return trip from Mexico to Spain in 1563. The king gladly assented to Menéndez' pleas.

Then, like a shot out of the blue, an astounding bit of intelligence was received at the court of King Philip II. In a shocking revelation, the Governor of Havana sent a letter by rapid courier to Philip II reporting that a French naval expedition under the command of René de Laudonnière had reached the mouth of the River of May, now known as the St. Johns River near present-day Jacksonville. Moreover, Philip II was informed that a second expedition was preparing to sail from France to reinforce him. While Laudonnière's expedition was short-lived, the French soldiers did manage to erect Fort Caroline at the mouth of the St. Johns before the second French fleet, under the command of Captain Jean Ribault, arrived to reinforce them. These French incursions, however, were not merely colonial ventures supported on political and economic grounds. There was a complex religious dimension attached to these latest French and Spanish ventures in North America.

The French, who were now settling and charting the Northeast coast of Florida were known as Huguenots. They were the religious followers of the French reformation theologian John Calvin. Following Martin Luther's initiation of the Protestant Reformation in 1517, Calvin began to expand on Luther's ideas and began to fundamentally reject such claims as papal authority and justification by faith alone. Needless to say, such notions did not sit so well with the Catholic party in France and, for that matter, in Catholic Spain. By 1562, the first of what were known as the bloody "Wars of Religion" (or Huguenot Wars) had begun in France and spread throughout Europe. Catholics and Protestants engaged in grisly campaigns in Europe and, by extension, in the American colonies of the European powers. Now, there was added impetus for the Spanish Crown to get Menéndez and his soldiers to the New World. While ghastly and grotesque in its earliest manifestation, religion would once again find itself intertwined with the colonial explorations of La Florida.

ABOVE: *Pedro Menéndez de Aviles, Primer Adelantado y Conquistador de la Florida. His expedition sighted the coast of Florida near present-day St. Augustine, on August 28, 1565.*

With renewed monetary support from the Crown, Menéndez's fleet of 20 ships and 2,600 men sailed from the port of Cadíz in Southwest Spain on June 29, 1565. On board were 11 Franciscan friars, eight Jesuit priests, and some Spanish diocesan priests. By the time the beleaguered fleet landed in Puerto Rico, there were only five ships left. Nevertheless, it was decided by Menéndez to set sail for Florida at once. On August 28, 1565, the fleet caught sight of land off Cape Canaveral, near the same spot where Juan Ponce had sighted land 52 years earlier. The date was the Catholic feast day celebrating the life of Saint Augustine, the famed Doctor of the Church and Bishop of Hippo, in North Africa. A Latin hymn of praise and thanksgiving usually recited on feast days, the *Te Deum*, was sung aboard the Spanish ships. On September 8, 1565, after having sailed up the coast, the Menéndez expedition decided to put ashore to the west of Anastasia Island. They named the spot St. Augustine.

As the landing took place, cannons fired, the colors of Castile were unfurled, and the new land was claimed for the King of Spain. Father López then offered a Holy Mass of thanksgiving. It was the

UPPER RIGHT: *Some of the artifacts, such as this bronze cross, found in the church at the Mission San Luis in Tallahassee, may be evidence of the Apalachee's religious conversion and their adoption of Christian symbols.*

BELOW: *1593 Spanish map, earliest demarcation of the Mission Nombre de Dios, St. Augustine. "Indian Village Nombre de Dios".*

first parish Mass, so to speak, in what was to become the United States. It also marked the first authenticated instance of a Roman Catholic community gathering together on the Atlantic Seaboard to celebrate the rites of Christian worship. At the place where Mass was celebrated, Father López established the Mission of Nombre de Dios, or Name of God, because they claimed the land in God's name. Due to its historic significance, the site of the first Holy Mass in the United States has become known in modern times as "America's Most Sacred Acre."

The landing at St. Augustine took place 55 years before the landing of the Puritan Pilgrims at Plymouth Rock, 40 years before the British settled the colony of Jamestown, and more than 210 years before the American Revolution. It was at Nombre de Dios that the first Christian thanksgiving celebration in a permanent European settlement was conducted. Long before turkey was basted and pumpkin pie was baked in New England, Catholic Christians were celebrating their religious heritage in what would later become the United States of America.

Today, the old mission grounds stand as a silent witness to America's Christian past. A rustic altar awakens the memory of Father López' first Mass. That first sacrifice is memorialized by a modern sculpture of Father López, arms raised and eyes skyward, which was created by the Croatian-American sculptor Ivan Mestrovic. Mestrovic is acknowledged as one of the finest sculptors of the 20th century. The mission chapel, now known as the Shrine

BELOW: *"The First Mass" celebrated in St. Augustine from an oil painting in the Spanish Cathedral. The painting hung in the Cathedral prior to the 1887 fire.*

ABOVE: *Our Lady of La Leche Chapel at Mission Nombre de Dios, St. Augustine. The first chapel building was erected in1615. It fell victim to times of war, pirates and storms with the last reconstruction in 1918.*

BELOW: *A 1587 Bible once belonging to the Pons Family of St. Augustine.*

of Nuestra Senora de la Leche y Buen Parto, or Our Lady of the Milk, takes its ancient name from interesting transcontinental circumstances.

On a September morning in Spain in 1598, a carved wooden statue of the Blessed Mother nursing the Christ Child was lifted from a church in Madrid by a drunken soldier. Holding the 10-inch statue aloft and profaning its significance in the streets of Madrid, the soldier was approached by a pious Spanish laborer who could no longer bear the public desecration of Our Lady's image. The holy man confronted the inebriated infantryman and asked for the statue courteously. Short of fisticuffs, the soldier sold the statue to the man for 50 Spanish maravidoses. The man took the statue to his home, where he and his wife became devoted to the image.

When the wife of the pious man became sick during her first pregnancy, the image of the nursing Mother inspired her with courage and infinite maternal love. After fervent prayer, the woman gave birth to a healthy child and recovered quickly from her illness. The devotion to the Nursing Mother of Jesus elicited a special spiritual connection for ill and pregnant women. On April 17, 1602, King Philip III assisted in installing the couple's statue in a shrine attached to St. Martin's monastery in Madrid. Quickly, a devotion to the Nursing Mother spread throughout the Spanish countryside.

It is not surprising then that the Spanish who flowed into St. Augustine after 1602 carried this devotion with them. Nor is it exceptional that the small chapel at the Mission Nombre de Dios would come to be called the Shrine of Our Lady of the Milk. In recent times, the shrine has become an inspiration for mothers who, much like the Spanish mother in Madrid in 1598, choose to promote the spiritual sanctity and dignity of their unborn children regardless of the human cost.

However, to the native inhabitants of Florida, these new rites were foreign as well as fascinating. After the 1565 landing, a "golden era" of Spanish missionary activity was inaugurated. The men who would carry out the spiritual conquest of North America were members of the Order of Saint Francis of Assisi, commonly known as the Franciscans, and the members of the Society of Jesus, the Jesuits. The Society of Jesus was founded in 1534 and known throughout Europe for its missionary and educational expertise. The first Jesuits arrived in St. Augustine in April of 1566. Fathers Juan Rogel and Brother Francisco Villareal were accompanied by Florida's first Jesuit martyr, Father Pedro Martínez.

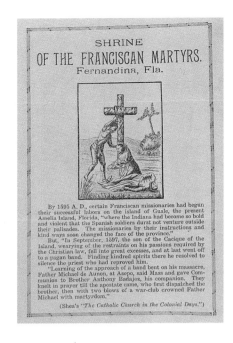

SHRINE
OF THE FRANCISCAN MARTYRS.
Fernandina, Fla.

By 1595 A. D., certain Franciscan missionaries had begun their successful labors on the island of Guale, the present Amelia Island, Florida, "where the Indians had become so bold and violent that the Spanish soldiers durst not venture outside their palisades. The missionaries by their instructions and kind ways soon changed the face of the province."
But, "In September, 1597, the son of the Cacique of the Island, wearying of the restraints on his passions required by the Christian law, fell into great excesses, and at last went off to a pagan band. Finding kindred spirits there he resolved to silence the priest who had reproved him.
"Learning of the approach of a band bent on his massacre, Father Michael de Aunon, at Asopo, said Mass and gave Communion to Brother Anthony Badajoz, his companion. They knelt in prayer till the apostate came, who first dispatched the brother, then with two blows of a war-club crowned Father Michael with martyrdom."
(Shea's "The Catholic Church in the Colonial Days.")

Of course, these first Jesuits faced many hardships in their work with the Native Americans. They approached their work of conversion from a purely European point of view. And while they stressed points of similarity between native culture and religion, they were also known to "browbeat" the natives into acceding to Catholic doctrine, particularly on points such as polygamy, trial marriage, and native dress. Father Martínez, while known as a man of great endurance, was nonetheless slain on Amelia Island while clutching his crucifix and reciting a litany of the saints. In many places the Jesuits were met with resistance. The plight of Father Martínez simply accentuated the horrors of missionary living. Moreover, Spanish soldiers were becoming wary of the natives and began to carry out some military reprisals. By 1572, the Jesuits had enough. Pulling out from Florida, they left new missionary ventures to their brothers of the brown habit, the Order of Friars Minor of Saint Francis of Assisi.

*BELOW: The church at San Luis near Tallahassee has been reconstructed to resemble its early beginnings. Approximately 50 by 110 feet, the church was equal in size to the church in St. Augustine. Inside the entrance to the left is the baptistry, where the limestone base of the font was found intact.*

The first Franciscans landed in Florida in 1573, but little is known of their work until 1594. Founded in Italy in 1209, they were known for their preaching and for their outreach to non-Christians. The Franciscans were dedicated to living the vow of poverty while they guided their daily lives by the

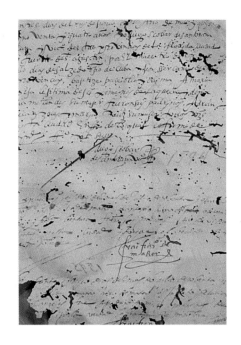

Rule of Saint Francis, the spiritual guidebook of Franciscan piety. As early as the 1580s the Franciscans began to show a remarkable outreach to the Timucua natives who inhabited the region from St. Augustine up to and around the St. Johns River near modern Jacksonville. In fact, the Mission Nombre de Dios became a center of Timucuan religious work. But all was not harmonious between the Franciscans and the Native Americans. Just as the Jesuits before them met with hostility, so too did the Franciscans in 1597. Father Pedro de Corpa of Tolamato Mission was so "unsparing in his harsh rebukes" to the natives that they rose up against him. The frank Franciscan was slain at the foot of his mission altar. Chopping off the priest's head, the natives carried their severed trophy atop a high pole and ransacked four other Franciscan missions. The "Indian Uprising of 1597" sent a chill over all further missionary efforts.

A breakthrough occurred in 1614, when Franciscan missionary Francisco Pareja translated a dictionary and grammar book to the Timucuan language. Spurred on by better communication, over time the Timucua came to embrace Catholicism sincerely. In 1617, when Jesuit Father Luis Lecson visited St. Augustine as a commissioner for the Bishop of Santiago de Cuba, he was duly impressed with the number of Native American conversions. In his report it is stated that he "inspected the records and the Church of St. Augustine and found everything clean and in good order."

Over the next decade, missionary efforts progressed smoothly so that by 1630, 20,000 natives had been baptized. The natives were also becoming allied to their Franciscan teachers. During a native revolt against the settlers in 1656, many Spanish were harmed while the Franciscans were left untouched. The integration of the natives into church life and practice was a central theme of the Diocesan Synod, or conference, held in Santiago, Cuba in 1684. At that time,

ABOVE: *The first page of the St. Augustine Parish Register of Baptisms, the oldest permanent record in the United States dated June 10, 1594.*

RIGHT: *For the residents at San Luis Mission, the 17th-century church was the most visible symbol of Christianity. Archaeological research has revealed that the church was a wooden building faced with vertical plants. Its thatched roof was supported by massive posts.*

St. Augustine was administered as a part of the Diocese of Santiago de Cuba. Special exemptions for fasting and abstinence were granted to the natives because the Franciscan fathers did not want to discourage them and this portion of the faith was still inadequately explained. The synod did, however, emphatically point out the excellent missionary work which was being undertaken in Florida.

Indeed, during the 135 years of Florida's missionary "golden age," much work had taken place. Between 1567 and 1705 nearly 80 mission centers, some 60 with churches, had been established. The Franciscans were serving more than 11 distinct native tribes. The Christianization of Florida, however, could not shake the long inheritance of the European Wars of Religion.

In 1702, British colonists centered at Charleston, began to raid southward into Spanish Florida. Governor James Moore of South Carolina sent raiding parties to attack the coastal missions. Moving as far south as St. Augustine, Moore's forces captured and burned all the missions, schools, and convents surrounding the city. Two Franciscans were killed in the raid. The prized Franciscan library in St. Augustine, containing rare Latin and Greek texts, was torched. By 1705, most of the Franciscan mission stations in Florida had been reduced to rubble. Any attempt to revive the mission system met with sad results. British claims in North Carolina and Georgia offered a constant threat to new initiatives. Yet, if the raids of the early 18th century symbolized the demolition of the missions in Florida, they also exemplified how desperately the Catholics of St. Augustine relied on the civil authorities for protection and support. When the British attacked Florida in 1705, missionaries and surrounding villagers fled to the Castillo de San Marco, the Spanish fort at St. Augustine, for protection.

Original construction on the Castle of St. Mark was begun as early as 1672. Prior to the new fort, the Spanish had been relying on a series of wooden forts which were susceptible to ambush and fire. One of the places where the Spanish would have assembled during the British raids was a small room on the north side of the castillo.

UPPER LEFT: *Originally a church of the Jesuits, construction of the Cathedral of Havana was begun in 1656 and completed in 1724. While Florida was served from the Cathedral of Santiago de Cuba from 1565-1787, Havana Cathedral was the episcopal seat from 1787-1793.*

BELOW: *This quartz crystal cross was found in the church at San Luis Mission. Archaeologists believe the cross was made by a native artisan.*

ABOVE: *A 1702 copy of the Rule of Saint Francis thought to have been used by Franciscan Friars who served more than 11 distinct native tribes in Florida between 1567 and 1705.*

BELOW: *Interior view of the military Chapel at the Castillo de San Marcos in St. Augustine.*

Building 14 of the Castillo de San Marcos, according to Spanish colonial records, was designated as the military chapel. Today, the room is musty, bare, and notoriously damp. The only trace of its Catholic past is a concave niche above where the altar used to stand and the remnants of a holy water font. In the niche, it is reported, an image of Saint Mark, the patron of the fort, used to hang. Construction of the chapel began as early as 1683. The altar, the printing of Saint Mark, an altar cloth of fine linen, and a missal on its stand decorated the interior. A bell for summoning soldiers to Mass, a storage chest, and a small pot for the holy water completed the supplies of the chapel. By 1753, Mass was celebrated at the fort on holy days by a military chaplain. Daily Mass was not offered in the fort because the thriving Mission Nombre de Dios was right next door. When Mass was celebrated, the chapel offered an intimate setting for liturgy.

One can imagine that a sense of community, banded together by military mission and Spanish national pride, led to a true feeling of single purpose. The Spanish soldiers and their families, so far from home, sweltering in heat and constantly subjected to attack from land and sea, took solace in the prayerful atmosphere of the small chapel. Moreover, the military chapel came to exemplify the strong bond between church and state as it existed during the Spanish period. This special bond had been tried in the wilderness of Florida since the early 16th century, and as the 18th century dawned over the marshes of La Florida, new political challenges would test the Spanish church-state connection to an even greater degree.

# A Farewell To Florida

## 1 7 6 3 - 1 8 2 1

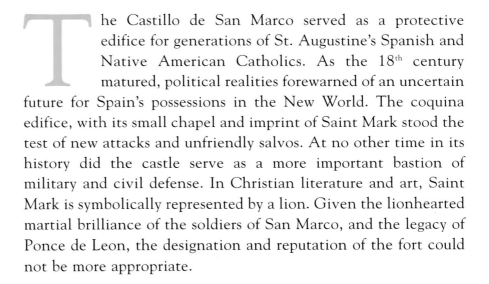

"At the time of the cession most of the Spanish inhabitants remained, but the arbitrary and rapacious conduct of the first English commander led to a general emigration. The unfinished walls of the parish church, the church at Tolemato, the sole remnant of the Indian towns near the city, the Franciscan convent and the temporary parish church, and a steeple of a church west of the town alone remained to betoken the Catholic occupation."

— Captain Bernard Romans, A Concise Natural History of East and West Florida, 1775

LEFT: *Castillo de San Marcos, the oldest fort in the United States, is located on Matanzas Bay in St. Augustine circa 1891.*

The Castillo de San Marco served as a protective edifice for generations of St. Augustine's Spanish and Native American Catholics. As the 18th century matured, political realities forewarned of an uncertain future for Spain's possessions in the New World. The coquina edifice, with its small chapel and imprint of Saint Mark stood the test of new attacks and unfriendly salvos. At no other time in its history did the castle serve as a more important bastion of military and civil defense. In Christian literature and art, Saint Mark is symbolically represented by a lion. Given the lionhearted martial brilliance of the soldiers of San Marco, and the legacy of Ponce de Leon, the designation and reputation of the fort could not be more appropriate.

In fact, Moore's raids from the Carolinas were just precursors of future battles. On the high seas, political tensions, fueled by ever-present religious discord, initiated some of the more peculiar events of Spanish rule in Florida. In the mid-18th century, Hispano-British relations continued to run hot due to competing commercial interests in the Caribbean. Smugglers, pirates, and buccaneers sailed the main preying on cargo ships laden with tribute for the Kings of Europe and England. In 1739, a British corsair was stopped and searched by the indomitable Spaniard Juan de Leon Fandino. The commander of the British vessel, Robert Jenkins, argued with Fandino and the confrontation came to blows. A fight aboard ships ensued. Spaniards swung from the halyards with sabers held high. In the midst of the fray, Fandino cornered Jenkins and with one swipe of his scimitar, lopped off the Englishman's ear. "Take this ear to your English King and tell him that I would do the same to him!" When shipmaster Jenkins returned to England, he thrust his severed ear down on a table at the House of Commons and dared Prime Minister Robert Walpole to declare war on Spain. The "War of Jenkins Ear" had considerable ramifications for citizens of St. Augustine.

In 1740, the British commissioned General James Oglethorpe, founder of the royal colony of Georgia, to attack the Spanish at St. Augustine. In May of 1740, Oglethorpe reached the northern outskirts of St. Augustine. Not long after, six Spanish galleys arrived at Mantazas Bay, near St. Augustine. The captain of the expedition was none other than Fandino, the irascible Spaniard who had slashed Jenkins' ear and started the war in the first place. With Oglethorpe closing in, provisions were made at St. Augustine to brace for another siege. This time, the fortifications were extended to include the Mission Nombre de Dios, adjacent to the fort. The "sacred acre" abruptly turned into a war zone. Barricades were thrown up and a military perimeter was established by the Catholic Yamassee natives who manned the site. Spanish soldiers occupied the forward bulwarks, just steps away from the mission church.

ABOVE: *East Florida currency representing 12-1/2 cents in the late 18th century.*

The British siege lasted 38 days. Again, the British were unable to penetrate the fort of St. Mark. When two Spanish warships ran the British blockade and came to the aid of the imperiled Spaniards, Oglethorpe raised the flag and withdrew northward into Georgia. Once again St. Augustine stood firm. The next 23 years would become the golden age of St. Augustine. During this period, Spanish customs and manners were woven into the fabric of the ancient city's way of life. Significant colonial buildings were constructed for St. Augustine's 3,000 inhabitants. Ever present, the Roman Catholic Church continued its spiritual life unencumbered by outside religious and political threats, a remarkable accomplishment considering that to the north, the French and Indian War was raging with a vengeance.

This new colonial war was, like others before it, an extension of a European conflict — this one known as the Seven Years War. Spain, worried deeply about British influence over North America, sided with the French in 1761. In the end, this strategic decision turned out to be a catastrophe. British naval superiority held the day and France exited from North America, ceding Canada to the British and requiring Spain, through the Treaty of Paris of 1763, to give up Florida to the English Crown. After almost 200 years, Spain was forced to relinquish on paper what she had defended most valorously with her blood. But this political reality now left the Roman Catholic Church in Florida in a quandary. How would the new captors view the Catholic religion? Would tolerance reign, or would the blood of many years be so thick as to obscure the Catholic gains of centuries?

On July 20, 1763, the first contingent of British Red Coats marched through the Plaza de la Constitución in St. Augustine. All together, there were 3,096 Spanish soldiers and citizens watching the parade of polished boots and shiny brass. The Spanish flag was lowered at the venerable Castillo de San Marcos, and the Union Jack was ceremoniously raised. Building 14, the military chapel, was converted into a vault for the British treasury. The first Spanish period of Florida history had ended. For their part, the British did promise "liberty of the Catholic religion...so far as the laws of Great Britain permit," but many Spaniards saw this as a token offer to a vanquished people. Moreover, as compensation, King Charles III of Spain offered free land and a home in Cuba or Mexico to any Floridians who wanted to resettle. With the prospect of persecution in Florida or a free home in other lands, the Spanish inhabitants of Florida began packing-up their belongings to head south en masse toward more peaceful shores.

The parish records of St. Augustine, dating back to 1594, were carefully stowed for the trip to Santiago de Cuba, where they would remain for the next 143 years. Meanwhile, the parish priests and Franciscans readied to move with their entire spiritual community to Cuba, thus abandoning Florida of all clerical leadership. By 1764, there were no more than eight Catholic laymen, and not one priest, in all of Florida.

In a last-ditch effort, the Spanish attempted to convey church property in Florida to private Catholic hands, thus circumventing British confiscation. The Franciscans attempted to sell all of their considerable lands to a wealthy Anglo-Catholic from South Carolina, John Gordon. In return, Gordon promised to hold the lands in abeyance until a new political situation arose. Perhaps it was wishful thinking, or merely a foreshadowing of the property disputes that would rock Florida Catholicism in the 19th and 20th centuries, but the British would have nothing of this scheme. The English argued that the Franciscans could not sell lands independently because of their contractual tie to the Spanish Crown. All Catholic lands, including the chapel of Neustra Senora de la Leche, had to be surrendered to the British. By 1772, all

TOP LEFT: *Portrait of the first Governor of East Florida, British General James Grant, 1764-1771.*

Catholic churches, chapels and lands had been converted to use by the Church of England. The spiritual and physical eradication of Catholic life in Florida was complete.

Yet out of the ashes of ecclesiastical scorched earth policy, a voice rose in the wilderness. In an improbable tale of endurance and adaptation, a vigorous Catholic priest from the beautiful Spanish Island of Minorca was called upon to keep the Catholic faith alive on Florida's coasts. The priest's name was Father Pedro Camps and his story is one of simple faith and impossible odds.

In 1767, the Scottish financier, surgeon, and entrepreneur Andrew Turnbull decided that British Florida afforded a prime location for the establishment of silk factories and cotton plantations. Somewhat comparable to Menéndez' dreams for Florida wealth 200 years earlier, Turnbull saw Florida as his unexploited "land of the future," and worked to establish a small colony with government help. His first order of business was to contract non-free laborers, indentured servants as they were called, for his new indigo mills. At the end of their indenture, the workers would be given free land to build their homes in Florida. Setting-up headquarters at the Port of Mahon on the Island of Minorca, Turnbull succeeded in conscripting 1,403 Minorcans, Greeks, and Italians to work in his fields and factories. By a strange twist of fate, Turnbull's wife, who was a Roman Catholic, insisted to her husband that the predominantly Catholic group of Minorcans be accompanied by a priest on their journey to Florida. At the time, Father Pedro Camps was 38 years old and held a doctorate in theology from the University of Mallorca. He agreed, with the approval of the Holy See at Rome, to accompany the ragtag group of Catholic immigrants to Florida's sunny shores.

ABOVE LEFT: *St. George Street in St. Augustine with its overhanging balconies and narrow path is characteristic of the Oldest American City. At left is the site of the first Minorcan Chapel of Father Pedro Camps.*

The group of Minorcan men and women arrived at Mosquito Inlet. They called their settlement New Smyrna, and began clearing the land to build Turnbull's enterprises. Much like earlier European undertakings in Florida, nature began to bear down on the immigrants. Heat, mosquito infestations, and a lack of food all took their toll. By 1768, a group of 300 Italians rioted; Turnbull executed two ringleaders and stopped the mutiny. Throughout, Father Camps celebrated Mass in a crude shack he named St. Peter's Church, ministered to his flock, gave constant consolation, and instructed the youth. For as much comfort as he provided, even the humble Father Camps was incensed to find out that in March of 1777, Andrew Turnbull refused to grant the Minorcans their freedom once the time of their indenture was up. Infuriated by this turn of events, the defiant group set out on foot to press their claim with the British Governor at St. Augustine. Along the way, Father Camps ministered to the sick, anointed the dying, and gave support to their quest.

When Governor Patrick Tonyn ruled in their favor, all Minorcans were released of their bond and Turnbull left Florida with his dreams of empire laid waste. Father Camps set up a new church in St. Augustine and began to minister to his flock there. The Minorcans became a permanent cultural component of the St. Augustine scene for generations to come. Perhaps the seaside town reminded them of home, but in any case their record of achievement mixed ever so delicately with the history of the town, forming what one historian has called a "Spanish and Balearic nucleus encrusted in Florida." But the Minorcan legacy of St. Augustine is as religious as it is historic. The poet William Cullen Bryant noticed this during the 19th century when he wrote A Tour in the Old South, a work which chronicled Minorcan culture in St. Augustine and paid particular attention to the Minorcan devotion to the Blessed Virgin Mary.

ABOVE: *Statue of Father Pedro Camps and the Minorcans of St. Augustine located in the courtyard of the Cathedral.*

RIGHT: *The Golden Book of the Minorcans, the sacramental register from 1768-1784, with the signature of Father Pedro Camps.*

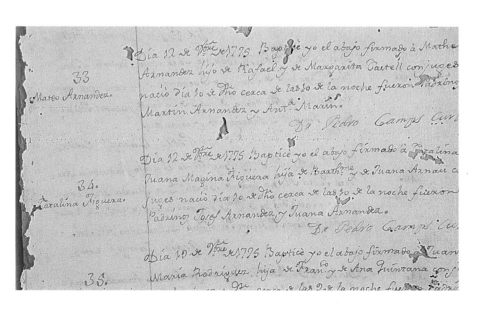

Indeed, the Blessed Mother may have blessed Father Camps in his work, but the fatigue of travel and the campaign for freedom clearly left the priest tired and worn-out.

If the Catholic Church was to progress in Florida, it needed to be reinvigorated with new clerical leadership. To this end, Father Camps wrote to the Bishop of Santiago de Cuba, requesting new recruits. In reply, Bishop Santiago José Echeverría y Elguezúa responded that he would dispatch two secular priests for service in the British colony.

Bishop Echeverría recruited the two young men from the famed Pontifical University of Salamanca in Spain. Founded in the 12th century, by 1422 it ranked as one of the four great universities of the world. Now Florida would be the beneficiary of more men of letters. The two missionaries were Father Thomas Hassett and Father Michael O'Reilly, graduates of Salamanca's College of Irish Nobles. They were both strapping men in their mid-20s, and they were both natives of Longford, Ireland. Bishop Echeverría chose wisely. Both men had engaging personalities, sincere faith, and were bilingual.

Try as they might, political events worked to delay the two men from landing in Florida. By 1779, the two theologians found themselves stranded in Cuba. The American Revolution was raging along the North Atlantic coast of the United States. Spain, which had thrown in her lot with the Americans, was at war with the British Navy in the Carribean. As the British faced a losing battle in the American War of Independence, new plans had to be made for its colony in Florida. In 1783, Britain confirmed Florida's cession back to Spain and in 1784 evacuated its colonies. Almost like the Spanish 20 years earlier, the British subjects packed their belongings, transferred lands, and solemnly boarded their ships for friendlier vistas. The "Second Spanish Period" was about to dawn on St. Augustine and its Catholic inhabitants.

This latest change, however, did not occur as drastically as the end of the First Spanish Period in 1763. The new Spanish were convinced that commerce, and not necessarily the Cross, would turn Florida into a profitable enterprise. Whereas previously the mission system was setup alongside the civil and military establishment, this time it was open trade and religious toleration that was encouraged. Formerly, only devout Catholics were free to operate in Florida. Now, Catholics as well as Lutherans, and a remnant of Anglicans, found themselves living together. Protestant farmers who had migrated from the Carolinas and Georgia now lived in freedom and toleration. King Charles III issued an edict that the Catholic Church need not require English

**A PRIEST FOR LIBERATION**

Father Felix (Juan) Varela, a candidate for sainthood, was a Cuban-born priest who grew up in St. Augustine in the late 1700s. He has been described as a champion of the poor and a strong promoter of Cuba's independence from Spain.

Born in Cuba in 1788, Varela was orphaned at an early age. He was sent to live with his mother's brother, Bartolome Morales, who was governor of St. Augustine.

He returned to Havana to study for the priesthood. Father Varela was ordained in 1811 and elected to to the Spanish parliament in Havana in 1821. Published reports say that Varela, while in Spain, was so outspoken on his views for Cuba's independence that he was expelled from Spain. He couldn't return to Cuba because it was a Spanish territory, so he went to New York where he eventually became vicar general of the Archdiocese of New York.

In 1851, in failing health, Father Varela retired to St. Augustine, where he died and was buried in 1853. He was reinterred in Havana in 1911 where a national shrine was built in his honor.

residents to embrace Catholicism, as in the First Spanish Period, but instead local parish priests were to "win them over by gentle preaching."

Ably suited for the task was the gentle Father Hassett, who arrived in St. Augustine in June of 1784. Immediately, he began to inspect the church and found it seriously lacking in accommodation for the Mass. Father Camp's small church by the City Gate, had been functioning since 1777. Soon, new quarters would be arranged in the upper story of the Old Bishop's House. Father O'Reilly was named assistant pastor of the new parish. Typical of his esteem for education, by 1787 Father Hassett had opened a small school for the Minorcan children of St. Augustine. Times were difficult, but the faith in Florida was making progress.

Organizationally, this progress was exemplified by new jurisdictional demarcations. As a Spanish colony from 1565 to 1763, Florida was placed under the ecclesiastical jurisdiction of the Archdiocese of Santiago de Cuba. In 1787, East Florida was placed under the jurisdiction of the new Diocese of San Cristóbal de Havana, Cuba. West Florida and Louisiana were placed under the administration of the Auxiliary Bishop Cyril of Barcelona, Spain. In 1788, Bishop Cyril visited West Florida and traveled overland to St. Augustine to visit with Father Hassett. During this visit, Bishop Cyril noticed that almost none of the African-Americans in the colony had been baptized. He warned Father Hassett that more had to be done to instruct them in the Roman Catholic faith. Soon, a new outreach of catechetical instruction was established for African slaves. This was the first structured educational program offered to African-Americans in Florida. Tragically, the rank injustice of slavery itself was hardly an open topic for theological debate. On the other hand, the fact that the church bell rang every Sunday afternoon for classes, must have given the West African slaves a sense of soulful worth, an understanding of God's love, and even a subtle sense of empowerment. The new outreach to African slaves did little to dispel the fact that this new era of Spanish authority was less than fruitful, both materially and spiritually. Very few of the new immigrants in Spanish Florida were adopting the faith of the Spanish. There were no new towns being developed and the Spanish were now beginning to come into conflict with the new government of the United States, which was eyeing Florida as a

ABOVE: *18th-century theology texts possibly used by Irish seminarians assigned to St. Augustine after ordination.*

BELOW: *Portrait of Dr. Andrew Turnbull who brought the Minorcans to Florida under a royal charter.*

potential territory. Furthermore, no new commerce was feeding the Spanish treasury. The government was becoming weaker and weaker. Father Hassett, usually long-suffering, began to refer to St. Augustine in his correspondence as "this miserable colony."

If there was one thing that Bishop Cyril's visit of 1788 brought to light, it was that the inhabitants of St. Augustine needed a real church. After five years of correspondence, the bishop decided that a plot of land west of St. George Street and north of the plaza should be purchased for a new church edifice. In 1793, there was a coquina house and an orange grove on the spot. The Spanish crown purchased the site for 697 pesos, and later that year a cornerstone was laid. Coquina from the original building was used to construct the new church as well as coquina from the ruins of Our Lady of La Leche Chapel on the grounds of Mission Nombre de Dios. The Spanish Crown undertook funding for the entire construction of the church. Because the Crown was weak and communications slow, the building was not completed until 1797. By that time poor Father Hassett was no longer in the diocese. In 1795, he was promoted to the post of Vicar General for the newly erected Diocese of Louisiana. Father O'Reilly, who had been assistant pastor, was moved up to pastor of the new church. "Old people still talk of this good priest with tears in their eyes," Bishop John Moore wrote of Father O'Reilly years later, "He was a man of rare scholarship and courtly manners." He would move Florida Catholicism into its first permanent church structure.

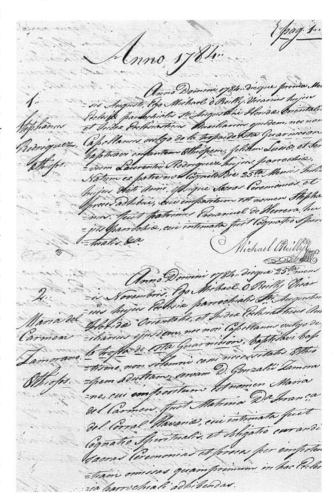

ABOVE: *This 1784 baptismal record is the first recorded Christening for an African-American in post-colonial Florida.*

On December 8, 1797, a long procession was formed on the plaza and the Blessed Sacrament was reverently placed in the tabernacle of the new church for the first time. Father O'Reilly led the procession through the Spanish-style facade and into the towering interior of the church. Above the main doors, a Spanish belfry narrowed to meet the sky. On one of the bells an inscription can be found, "Sancta Joseph, Ora Pro Nobis," Saint Joseph, Pray For Us. The date of the inscription was 1682. Below the belfry a small niche held a statue of Saint Augustine of Hippo, patron saint of the parish. On both sides of the main wooden altar were two smaller altars. One was dedicated to St. Joseph, while the other was dedicated to the Blessed Mother. For all their work, the Catholics of St. Augustine now had a church worthy of their Catholic legacy. Grounded in the past, it was a church that would thrust the Catholic community of St. Augustine into their own and

their nation's future. In the next century, this lovely church at St. Augustine would become the Cathedral Parish of all Florida.

By 1819, Florida was about to change hands one more time. Once again, political realities dictated change within the church. Since the turn of the century, citizens of East Florida had been petitioning the United States to purchase Florida because Seminole Native Americans were constantly raiding Florida's towns and then retreating across the Georgia border. Due to the fact that Spain's other colonies demanded a great deal of attention, Spain was willing to sell. On February 22, 1819, John Quincy Adams, Secretary of State for President James Monroe, and Luis de Onis of Spain signed a treaty that relinquished Florida to the United States for about $5 million. While the United States ratified the treaty quickly, it took two years for Spain to reach an accord.

By summer of 1821, St. Augustine had a new owner. In a ceremony that took place inside the castillo on July 10, 1821, the Star Spangled Banner was played and the American flag was raised on the plaza, directly across from the Spanish-style church. After lowering their flag, the Spanish said farewell to Florida. In their wake, they left a struggling missionary church, now part of a predominantly Protestant nation. Yet, instead of contracting into a defensive posture, the American experience would provide possibilities of freedom and expansion that even Spanish Florida could never have provided. The American chapter of Florida Catholic history would be its own "Golden Age."

*ABOVE: Luis Penalver y Cardenas, bishop of Louisiana and the Floridas. He administered Florida from New Orleans from 1793-1825. He was a priest of the Diocese of Havana.*

*BELOW: The City of St. Augustine was transfered from Spain to the United States on July 10, 1821 as depicted in this painting of Castillo de San Marcos by James Calvert Smith.*

# Coming of Age

## 1 8 2 1 - 1 8 7 7

*"The Bishop has had no time yet to visit his diocese. St. Augustine has a large majority of Catholics, and is in fact a Catholic town. It has a delightful climate, remarkably healthy; the land which can be had in its vicinity for one or two dollars per acre will repay the industrious Catholic settler who comes with moderate capital. The Indian War having been brought to a close, it is expected that Florida will be settled rapidly."*

— Bishop Augustin Verot, Sadlier's Catholic Directory, 1859.

ABOVE: *The original seal of the State of Florida.*

LEFT: *The City Gate of St. Augustine, a national monument.*

The growth of the Catholic Church in Florida paralleled the rise of America as a new Republic. From 1814 to 1818, significant military operations were conducted against the Native Americans by General Andrew Jackson. One year after America took possession of Florida, the land was designated a U.S. territory and William P. Duval was appointed its first governor. But as the Spanish ships sailed out of Matanzas Inlet in 1821, they left behind perhaps 400 Catholics in St. Augustine. There were about 100 Catholics living in and around the St. Johns River and another 100 living on Amelia Island. These true believers and final survivors were not only left behind by the Spanish, but were increasingly being tossed about by the church too. When America took over in Florida, Rome's eccesiastical authorities were somewhat confused as how to proceed. From 1819 to 1823 the Florida lands were under the jurisdiction of Bishop William Louis Dubourg of New Orleans. Dubourg never visited Florida, and by 1823 he came into conflict with the bishop of the newly erected Diocese of Charleston, Bishop John England, who also claimed authority over East and West Florida. Dueling bishops seldom make life easy for their flocks. Between 1819 and 1825 both bishops, on various occasions, claimed jurisdiction over a land they had never seen. Florida Catholics simply watched and prayed.

Soon, it was Bishop England who began to assert the rights of Catholics in Florida. In 1825, when the new United States Commissioner in St. Augustine informed the Catholics of the town that the government would soon take over all church property in Florida, a cry for help was sent to Charleston. Straight away, Bishop England appealed to President James Monroe. The president, in turn, referred the matter to the Secretary of State, John Quincy Adams. After acquainting himself with the issues, Adams relayed a message to the authorities in St. Augustine that it was not the original intention of the United States in the Adams-Onis Treaty to confiscate the church property in Florida. After receiving word from Adams, government clerks in St. Augustine backed off in their legal showdown with the Catholic community. John Quincy Adams, soon to be elected the sixth president of the United States, saved Florida Catholicism!

The church property dispute hammered home to the ecclesiastical authorities in Rome that real organization needed to be in place in Florida. In 1825, Rome established the Vicariate Apostolic of Florida and the Alabamas. A Vicariate Apostolic is a region where the structured hierarchy of the church has not yet been established and is under the immediate jurisdiction of a nearby bishop nominated by the pope. On this occasion, the pope chose Bishop Michael Portier, a Frenchman. Portier was a close friend of Bishop Dubourg of New Orleans, and at age 35, his youth and vigor helped him to traverse the new vicariate. In 1827, the vicar was ordered to visit his new jurisdiction and supply a report for the Roman authorities. His first stop was Pensacola, where Father Constantine Maenhaut was instructing Catholics and living an exemplary, priestly life. As Portier traveled toward St. Augustine, he noticed how well Protestants and Catholics seemed to be getting along. At many of his Masses, there were more Protestants in attendance than Catholics. After staying on in St. Augustine for a few months, all the while baptizing and hearing confessions, the new bishop left for New Orleans in September of 1827. He left the church in Florida in considerably better spiritual shape than when he found it.

Such spiritual growth is evidenced by the fact that lowly St. Augustine, the faraway port town of Florida, gave the first two American bishops to the Southern United States. Dominic Manucy was born December 20, 1823 in St. Augustine. Praying as a youth in the church of St. Augustine, he attended the Jesuit-run Spring Hill College in Alabama, and was ordained in 1850. In 1874, he was consecrated the Bishop of the Diocese of Brownsville, Texas, and, as one historian put it, "lived the life of a missionary bishop." The second Floridian to become a bishop was Anthony Dominic Pellicer. He, too, was a faithful son of Father Hassett's and O'Reilly's small church. Born in 1824, Pellicer also studied at Spring Hill College

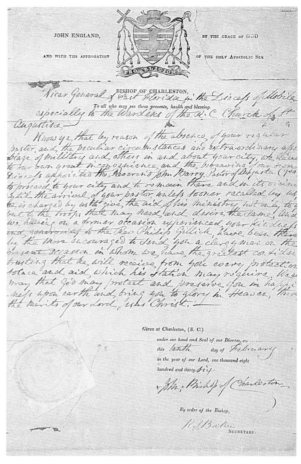

ABOVE: *A letter from John England, bishop of Charleston, South Carolina, agreeing to send a priest to St. Augustine during the Indian Wars in 1836.*

and was ordained in 1850. In 1874, he was consecrated to the Diocese of San Antonio, Texas. The sons of St. Augustine were reaping the graces and benefits of the missionaries who had come before them. It was the missionary work of Fathers Hassett and O'Reilly that planted the seeds of faithful leadership that grew in the hearts of two of St. Augustine's finest Catholic young men. The church in St. Augustine was small, but the power of its spirit was great indeed.

As the church grew in faith and spirit, so too, did Florida. In 1845, Florida was made a state and the 27th star was placed on the flag of the United States. Noticing this move, the Catholic church deemed it advisable to reconsider church organization in Florida one more time. In 1850, Florida was grafted onto the geographical boundaries of the newly created Diocese of Savannah. In 1857, looking forward to greater autonomy, Rome created the Vicariate Apostolate of Florida. Oversight for the evangelization and administration of this new territory was handed to a diminutive French seminary professor from Baltimore, Father Augustin Verot.

Jean Marcel-Pierre Augustin Verot was born on May 23, 1805 in Le Puy, France. The history of the Catholic Church in Le Puy was one of great dignity and fame. Charlemagne visited twice during the eighth century. Saint Anthony of Padua, Saint Dominic, and Saint Hugh of Grenoble all traveled to Le Puy to pray at its great cathedral which dates from the fifth century. Of course, the young Augustin Verot could not help but pray in the famed Cathedral of Le Puy, rising as it did from the highest precipice in the city. As a young man, praying fervently in the picturesque cloister of the cathedral overlooking the Loire Valley, Verot felt the call of God and the call of the ages. He answered his call by joining the Order of the Priests of Saint Sulpice, a group of diocesan priests who lived a spirit of priestly renewal in various seminaries and parishes. This calling to the vineyards of faith, emanating as it did on a hilltop in Le Puy, would ultimately mean great things and many spiritual benefits for the church in Florida. It was when Augustin entered the Sulpician novitiate in Paris that he found out that the order had a missionary seminary in a far-off land across the sea, the United States of America.

Willa Cather, the award-winning Catholic author of the 20th century, wrote in Death Comes for the Archbishop that in the early French missionary bishops there was something "well-bred and distinguished...something fearless and fine." These same attributes applied to Augustin Verot. After spending 27 years at St. Mary's Seminary in Baltimore teaching science, philosophy and theology,

ABOVE: *Bishop Anthony Dominic Pellicer (above), and Bishop Dominic Manucy, were born in St. Augustine. Both were named bishops on the same day in 1874.*

Verot was nominated Vicar Apostolic of Florida on December 11, 1857. Consecrated in Baltimore by Archbishop Francis P. Kenrick, Verot arrived in St. Augustine in 1858 and found the church there in a "disheartening" state.

Regardless of spiritual stamina, the fact was that there were only three priests in all of Florida in 1858; two in St. Augustine and one in Jacksonville. Mission chapels were in operation at Mandarin, Palatka, Mayport, Fernandina, and Middleburg. The mission on Key West was so far south that coverage was spotty. In total, there were 1,328 Catholics in all of Florida. And somewhat surprisingly to outside observers, more than one-third of the most devout Catholics were African American. But the new Vicar Apostolic knew he had his hands full if he ever wished to raise his ecclesiastical hinterland to the status of a true diocese. In fact, Verot had initially thought to decline Archbishop Kenrick's offer of the episcopacy. Verot was happiest surrounded by his seminary books and teacher's tools. "I would have refused at once, had I not been afraid of going against the will of God," he wrote to a fellow seminary professor in Baltimore. "The post being one of labor, privation, and suffering," he added. More certain words could not have been written. "To tell the truth plainly," he concluded rather tongue-in-cheek, "I think I deserve condolence much more than felicitations."

Lacking enough priests, and having to account for the prospective growth of the State of Florida, Verot knew that he needed help.

His first decision of weight, and probably one of the most historic decisions in Florida Catholic history, was his conclusion to head back to his beloved and faith-filled France to recruit priests to work in the "missions" of Florida. The new bishop set sail from New York for Havre in 1859 on the steamship Glasgow. But the going got rough even before the diminutive Frenchman took to the high seas. As soon as the good bishop arrived in New York, he was nearly mugged by a strange fellow who came to him "with great kindness and apparent zeal" to take him to his hotel. Eventually, he found himself "in a mean

LEFT: *Bishop Augustin Verot.*

ABOVE: *Bishop Verot's Coat of Arms.*

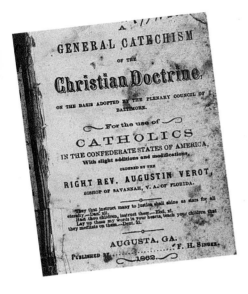

place on a small and wretched street." Bishop Verot "extricated" himself from the situation by boldly hailing a passing carriage. Later, he ruminated that it was "a wonder my baggage was not stolen." Even so, these tense moments failed to diminish his spirits. By his return trip he had recruited six priests from France to assist him with his new and increasingly heavier duties. In 1861, Verot's responsibilities were doubled when he was named bishop of Savannah while remaining Vicar Apostolic of Florida.

As grave as his parochial undertakings were in Florida and Georgia, new challenges loomed on the national scene. "The political horizon has become gloomy," Verot cautioned in a 1861 sermon at the Cathedral in St. Augustine. "Discord and disunity are rapidly spreading over the length and breadth of the land; horrors of war, and of the worst kind, civil war, are staring us in the face, and with the anticipation of evils yet worse to come." The great "War Between the States" was the most horrific campaign ever fought on American soil. Yet, amid the turbulence of canon and cacophony, Bishop Verot ministered to the faithful Catholics of Florida and Georgia with determination and Apostolic zeal.

In June of 1862 shouts of "The Yankees are coming!" echoed through the streets of St. Augustine. The doors of the Cathedral at St. Augustine burst open during Sunday Mass so that all Confederate soldiers could hear the news. As word spread, Bishop Verot warned the Sisters of Mercy of Providence, Rhode Island, who had been teaching African-American children there since 1859, that they should retreat to Columbus, Georgia, so as to remain out of harm's way. As resident "Yankees," the Sisters' safety was somewhat precarious now that war had been declared. In order to assure their safe passage, Bishop Verot made the trek to Georgia with them. The little band of Sisters and their bishop left St. Augustine in a torrential downpour, and, after having survived wading through a swamp and their caravan of mules careening over a hillside, were seized by Union troops. "We will fire into you," came words from the forest as soldiers materialized from the mist pointing their sabers at the lowly bishop and his sororal companions.

Since two of the Sisters were dark-complected natives of the Dominican Republic, Verot was accused of secretly transporting slave women to Georgia.

ABOVE: *Bishop Augustin Verot's catechism, 1862.*

BELOW: *Confederate soldiers in St. Augustine, 1861.*

After a brief inspection, a Federal officer approved of Verot's travel plans but strongly recommended that the sad party return to St. Augustine. The bishop kindly thanked the officer, disregarded his advice, and continued his course. Such determination in the face of overwhelming odds was characteristic of the little French Bishop of the South. The casual dismissal of the Union officer can be viewed as even more remarkable since Verot's support for slavery, on Biblical grounds, was well known throughout the South and to the Union troops particularly. Indeed, he had been branded the "Rebel Bishop" by his contemporaries.

However, Verot's rebellious attitude changed drastically after the war, when he changed his thinking on slavery and became one of the greatest proponents of education for the children of the "freedmen" of Georgia and Florida. In fact, Verot's determination and success in the area of African-American education marks the greatest involvement of Florida Catholicism in African-American advancement up to the Civil Rights era. To his credit, after the Civil War, Verot invited the Sisters of St. Joseph of Le Puy, France, to move to Florida and minister to the war-ravaged children. In Key West, the French Canadian Sisters of the Holy Name opened St. Francis Xavier School for African-Americans and enrolled 26 students.

With the dawn of a new decade, Bishop Verot headed to Europe to participate in the First Vatican Council. While in Rome, he articulated a novel concept to his fellow bishops, namely that people of African descent deserved full social and religious freedom. The Vicar of Florida and Bishop of Georgia also spoke out vociferously against the adoption of the teaching on Papal Infallibility, offering that it would undercut his ability to win converts to Catholicism in the predominantly Protestant South. True to his education in mathematics and physical science, he encouraged church fathers to seriously study scientific technology in its relation to society in general. It would be almost 100 years, not until Vatican II, when many of Verot's criticisms were accepted by the church on their own merit.

*ABOVE: Handmade items and lace-making tools used by the Sisters of St. Joseph from as early as 1867. The sisters sold the items to help finance their school for children of freed slaves in St. Augustine.*

In 1870, while he was in Rome for Vatican I, the Vatican's Sacred Consistorial Congregation informed him that they were considering the creation of a new diocese with its seat designated as St. Augustine. Compelled by missionary zeal, and his own deep attachment to the Florida wilderness, he asked to be given charge of America's newest and southernmost diocese. In 1870, he returned to St. Augustine to a grateful congregation and a renewed emphasis on fostering the growth of Catholicism in Florida.

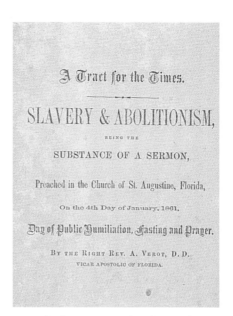

A Tract for the Times.

SLAVERY & ABOLITIONISM,

BEING THE

SUBSTANCE OF A SERMON,

Preached in the Church of St. Augustine, Florida,

On the 4th Day of January, 1861.

Day of Public Humiliation, Fasting and Prayer.

BY THE RIGHT REV. A. VEROT, D. D.
VICAR APOSTOLIC OF FLORIDA.

UPPER RIGHT: *A homily written by Bishop Verot and published in 1861.*

BELOW: *A French missionary chasuble, circa 1870 . The leather lining protected the rich needlework when the vestment was folded and stored in a saddlebag.*

Over the next six years, the bishop traveled incessantly throughout the diocese, conducting retreats and calling the first Diocesan Synod — an assembly of prelates gathered to decide upon matters pertaining to discipline and liturgy. His travels throughout the peninsula were legendary for their duration, hardship, and practical spirituality. He traveled long distances via horseback, slept outdoors in the wild, celebrated the Mass at Catholic homes scattered throughout the diocese, and led a life deprived of even the most rudimentary comforts. Consequently, Bishop Augustin Verot died on June 10, 1876 at St. Augustine shortly after he returned from a wide-ranging and fatiguing visitation of the diocese.

To this day, Verot is revered as a noble model of a Christian bishop. If his spirit can be quantified, then he may be recognized as the institutional founder of Florida Catholicism. By 1876 Verot had increased the number of priests in Florida from three to 11, the number of churches from six to 20 and provided the foundation for six parish schools. In addition, he enrolled two seminarians to study for the diocesan priesthood. At the time of his passing the Catholic population was at 10,000 souls. "Delicious oranges can now be obtained everywhere in Florida," the bishop wrote shortly before his death hoping to attract Catholic settlers to Florida, "Honest, industrious settlers, furnished with a reasonable capital, can scarcely meet with failure." Verot's optimism in Florida's future would be held in mind by the second bishop of the Diocese of Saint Augustine.

# Twenty-four Years Under the Sun

## 1 8 7 7 - 1 9 0 1

*"Under the present government there is no fear of physical persecution. All is in the moral side — but nothing can be said for the future. There is a great deal of bitterness against Catholicity, though not as much as a few years ago."*

— Rev. J. L. Hugon writing from the mission at Tallahassee to Bishop John Moore, 1878.

ABOVE: *19th-century French chalice, silver with gold lining.*

LEFT: *The Cathedral of St. Augustine, circa 1920.*

The years from the end of Reconstruction to the turn of the century were ones of expansion and hardship for the fledgling Diocese of St. Augustine. Lines of communication were still slow, vocations scarce, and tropical diseases rampant. Above it all, a worthy successor was needed to fill the giant shoes of Florida's first bishop. The new leader of the church in Florida needed to have a strong sense of the missionary role and a stout nature so as to bear up to the hardships of everyday life on the Florida peninsula. More than any single attribute, the new man had to possess an abundance of inner strength grounded in a firm prayer life and vibrant spirituality. By 1877, the Holy See believed that it had found the man; an Irishman whose entire personality and spiritual life was dedicated to advancing the mission of the Roman Catholic Church in "foreign parts."

John Moore was born in 1835 in Castletown, County Westmeath, Ireland. Growing up as a young boy, John could not have escaped the religious and historical bequest of his lineage. In 1649, Oliver Cromwell's new model army sacked the nearby town of Drogheda and struck fear into the newly enslaved Irish. As a young boy, the future Florida bishop played on the banks of the Boyne River, where, in 1690, the Roman Catholic King James II was soundly defeated by the army of William III of England. Time spent on the rolling hills of Westmeath helped to foster a sense of independence in young John Moore, a sense which he would draw on as tragedy struck close to home.

When the future bishop was only 14, William Moore, his beloved father, died and hard times descended on the family. In 1848, Moore and his sister made an oceangoing voyage to America, eventually settling in Charleston, South Carolina. At mid-century, Charleston was a bustling southern port town with a sizable Irish-Catholic population. As a teenager, Moore sensed a vocation to the priesthood and enrolled in Bishop Ignatius Reynolds minor seminary in Charleston. Moore distinguished himself in learning and maturity. With a watchful eye, Bishop Reynolds sent young John Moore to Europe for the completion of his education. His classical courses were taken at the College of Courbre in France. For theology he was sent to the Urban College of the Propaganda Fide in Rome, a natural choice for Moore since that college was specially geared for the training of priests in missionary lands. He was ordained in Rome in 1860 and shipped out for America just in time to arrive in Charleston as the bullets began to fly at Fort Sumter. Over the next 16 years, Moore served the Diocese of Charleston as one of its most revered pastors. His leadership abilities were recognized in 1871 when he was appointed Vicar General of the Charleston Diocese.

But Moore had been trained in the missionary spirit. Naturally, he welcomed the news that he received from Rome on February 16, 1877, when he was elected the second bishop of the Diocese of St. Augustine, the original land of the Spanish missionaries. Moore was consecrated in the Cathedral at Charleston on May 13 of that same year. Immediately, the new bishop traveled by horseback to his new episcopal home. As he rode into the city of St. Augustine, he took over jurisdiction of a diocese with 12 priests, a few scattered churches, and six struggling convents, all to serve a Catholic population of about 10,000.

The vastness of the flowered peninsula forced Moore to deal with administrative problems early on. Florida, 511 miles from Jacksonville in the north to Key West in the south, was a far-flung ecclesiastical enterprise in 1877. Consequently, Moore relied on his religious brothers in the faith to help in the evangelization of Florida. Moore virtually cordoned all of South Florida for administration by religious order priests. To Tampa and Miami he brought the Jesuits, while the Benedictine fathers were given claim

ABOVE: *John Moore, Bishop of Saint Augustine, 1877-1901.*

ABOVE: *The Third Plenary Council of Baltimore, 1884. Bishop Moore delivered the decrees of the Council to Pope Leo XIII in Rome.*

BELOW: *An 1882 parish census of St. Mary Star of the Sea, Key West. The census was signed by Father Felix Ghione, a Cuban-American missionary priest.*

to Florida's West Coast parishes. Eventually, both of these orders established fine Catholic educational institutions in Florida. The Benedictine's founded St. Leo College near Tampa, while the Society of Jesus established Tampa Jesuit High School. Moore also placed the church in Florida on solid ground by advancing the recruitment of seminarians, particularly seminarians from his native Ireland.

Administratively, it was Moore's persistence and resourcefulness that carried through many gains for the diocese throughout his tenure. Typical was a 1883 exchange in which Moore approached the U.S. government for permission to quarry some of the famous amalgamated seashell coquina stone from Anastasia Island near St. Augustine. The government had laid claim to the island's quarry since the end of the Civil War, but by 1883 the Cathedral of St. Augustine was in need of some repair. Since the cathedral was originally constructed using coquina stone, it seemed only natural that the material could be had for a market price. Unfortunately, the U.S. government was not about to sell the stone to the Catholic Church. After writing and getting pushed back by minions in the War Department in Washington, Moore wrote directly to the General of the U.S. Army, William Tecumseh Sherman.

If Sherman thought "war was hell," Moore must have thought that simple repairs to his church edifice were just as difficult. Since troops attached to Sherman's forces had already burned Immaculate

Conception Church in Jacksonville and St. Michael's Church in Fernandina Beach as far back as 1864, Sherman was probably not the best one to approach concerning Catholic interests. "I regret to inform you that there is no authority of law by which this request, commendable as it is, can be granted." "To enable this Department to grant your request," Sherman wrote in gruff military tone, "should require the special authorization of Congress." Sherman turned a simple request for building materials into an issue of church-state relations. Sherman, no fan of pinprick assaults, even signed his letter of declension "your obedient servant." Moore's plans for a reconstruction of his cathedral would have to wait. While Sherman's rebuff was a small setback, it could be stated that Bishop Moore's legacy is borne out more by the repercussions of adversity than the pleasantness of smooth sailing.

At about three o'clock in the morning on Tuesday, April 12, 1887, the sound of fire bells broke through the warm night time silence of St. Augustine. Sparks from the laundry building of the St. Augustine Hotel stealthily snaked along their wooden pathways. Soon an entire section of the city was illuminated with the deadly light. Sleepy-eyed citizens of the Ancient City reported that the stately old cathedral "went down in a tornado of destruction." A press reporter from Jacksonville arrived at 5:30 a.m. and surmised that the blaze registered "as a true public calamity due to the destruction of the Old Cathedral." A patron of the St. Augustine Hotel who witnessed the destruction that evening was James Renwick, a world-famous architect. Awakened from his slumber, Renwick gazed up as flames

UPPER RIGHT: *A view of St. Augustine from the bay after the fire of April 12, 1887 destroyed nearly all of downtown.*

BELOW: *A close-up of the Cathedral after the fire of 1887.*

engulfed the proud and sacred Spanish edifice. Then and there, he was determined to help the Catholics of St. Augustine rebuild their church. Immediately after the fire, Renwick volunteered his services as the sole designer of the new Cathedral of St. Augustine. The Catholics of the diocese could not have been more fortunate. Renwick, whose designs included St. Patrick's Cathedral in New York City and the Smithsonian Institution in Washington, D.C., was arguably the foremost architect of the era. Renwick's expertise was sorely needed for the magnificent building was gutted and charred to rubble. All that remained standing were the four walls originally constructed in 1797. It fell to Bishop Moore to reconstruct from scratch a cathedral worthy of its historic legacy. For months at a time, Moore, hat in hand, traveled to northern dioceses to beg for money. Each year he made stops at parishes in New York and Philadelphia to raise funds for a rebuilding project that would take more than 15 years to complete. His humility and resourcefulness were pushed to its limits. One bright spot in his quest for monetary assistance was the beneficence of Florida's gilded age captain of industry, Henry Flagler.

"What I especially like about the Catholic Church is this," the Florida railway magnate ruminated after meeting Bishop Moore, "she has only one boss." In the local church of St. Augustine, that "one boss" was Bishop Moore. Since their first meeting, it became clear that Moore's refined personality and nobility of character genuinely impressed Flagler. "There are two great institutions that never fail to accomplish what they set out to do," Flagler said after the fire and possibly commenting on Bishop Moore's solid persistence, "the Standard Oil Company and the Roman Catholic Church."

As a tribute to Moore, Flagler assisted in financing the building of the beautiful cathedral campanile. But as if things could not have gotten any worse, the year 1888 roared in like an annus horribilis, marked by Jacksonville's great yellow fever epidemic.

It was this latest challenge that brought out the best in Moore's application of practical Christianity. Instead of staying in the seaside town of St. Augustine, Bishop Moore rode head on into ground zero of the yellow fever explosion. "The city is now one yellow fever hospital,"

Moore wrote to his trusty assistant in St. Augustine, Father Edward Pace. In September of 1888, Moore trudged to Jacksonville's Immaculate Conception Church to take the reins from an obscure pastor, William J. Kenny, who succumbed to a relapse of the fever. "Father was stricken down two weeks ago, and I have come to do his work." Such humility on the part of this pioneer bishop is astounding. Not only did he deem it necessary as a priest to see that the sacraments were properly distributed, but he placed himself in harm's way in order to do so. "We have had regular yellow fever weather here for the past week," Moore wrote to Pace unknowingly foreshadowing his own bout with the dreaded disease, "rainy, sultry, clammy."

Two weeks later, Moore was stricken with the yellow fever. Eventually, he came out of the sickness in fine shape, mostly due to his unshakable constitution and, of course, a bit of therapeutic luck. But other men of the cloth were not so fortunate, a circumstance which underscored Moore's own sacrifice. All told, four priests perished at the hands of the epidemic, a considerable blow since it represented one quarter of all the priests in Florida at the time.

ABOVE: *An 1897 First National Bank Check from Bishop John Moore to Father William J. Kenny.*

BELOW: *The white winged Daughters of Charity came to the Diocese of Saint Augustine from Emmitsburg, Maryland in 1888. Their first mission was to serve as nurses during the Yellow Fever Epidemic. More than 4,000 Jacksonville residents were stricken with the fever and 437 died. In 1916, the Daughters of Charity purchased the DeSoto Sanatorium for $67,000 and renamed it St. Vincent's Hospital in honor of St. Vincent de Paul, the founder of the Daughters of Charity.*

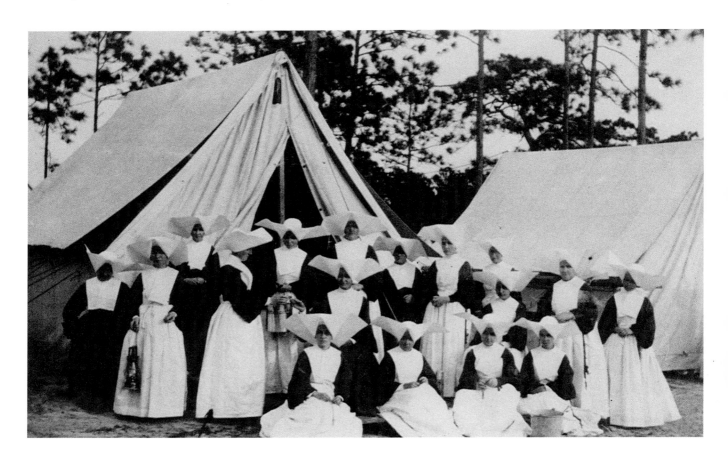

"How small everything seems in this world when it is compared with the self sacrifice of a pastor who gives up everything for the welfare and well-being of his people," commented the architect James Renwick. "I hope that the scourge will soon leave your diocese," Renwick wrote to Moore from his New York office in November of 1888, "and I sympathize with you in all your kind labors for the afflicted." Moore never publicly commented on his own travails with yellow fever. Surely, he believed that

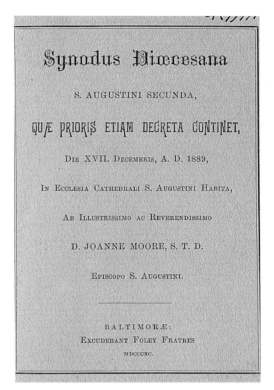

it was his episcopal duty to minister to his flock as they languished in fevered delirium.

But after almost 25 years as the leader of Florida's Catholic population, Moore's hearty character and prayerful will finally gave out. In August of 1899, the bishop fell to "paralysis," probably a stroke, while he was visiting friends in Wilkes-Barre, Pennsylvania. He spent the next two years in ill health in St. Augustine, but continued to make routine diocesan decisions up to his death two years later. His "final summons" came on July 30, 1901. Father William J. Kenny, who was at his side, stated that Moore passed on "just as a child goes to sleep." Given the adversity he faced over the years, Moore's advancement of the diocese was truly remarkable. Despite the epidemic and financial worries, he increased the number of priests to 31, placed more than 2,000 students in parochial schools, and rebuilt the Cathedral at St. Augustine. "He was unostentatious, without attracting attention to his humility," wrote Father Kenny, "He was simple in manner and easily approached."

The Florida Times-Union, Jacksonville's home newspaper, recalled Moore fondly, but also looked to the future as the Catholics of Florida were left rudderless to face a brand-new century. "Reverend W. J. Kenny of Jacksonville will remain in charge until the bishop's successor shall be duly selected," the paper reported. Intrigued by "Roman" rules, the newspaper speculated, "it is possible that Father Kenny may become the third Bishop of Florida...But this is merely supposition."

ABOVE: *Father Henry Clavreul at St. Joseph Church, Mandarin, in the late 1800s.*

UPPER RIGHT: *The second Synod of the Diocese of Saint Augustine occured in 1889 under the leadership of Bishop Moore.*

# Extending the Faith

## 1 9 0 2 - 1 9 1 3

*"I received your letter in due time last week whilst I was hard at work in Madison. My work there was very successful not only among non Catholics but also among Catholics, many of whom I rooted out of the holes they had crawled into. In all I think there are over 30 baptized Catholics there. There is a little church about four miles from the town which has not been used for some time, but I think I shall be able to put it to some use pretty soon if God will spare me."*

— Irish missionary Father Patrick J. Bresnahan letter to Bishop William J. Kenny, Dec. 14, 1904.

ABOVE: *A mosaic cross that belonged to Bishop William Kenny.*

LEFT: *Present-day interior view of Immaculate Conception Church, Jacksonville.*

When Father William J. Kenny was vested with the miter and crozier on May 18, 1902 by James Cardinal Gibbons, he had already been a loyal priest of the diocese for 23 years. The willingness of Cardinal Gibbons of Baltimore to conduct the ceremony was indeed an honor. But even more special was the fact that the priests of the diocese had recommended that Kenny become their new bishop upon the death of Bishop Moore. Certainly, Father Kenny was humbled by the unanimous backing of his peers, and the circumstance signaled a happy relationship between the priests and their bishop for years to come. Moreover, the choice of Father Kenny highlighted Kenny's esteem within the community. Members of both clergy and community all felt satisfied that the spiritual needs of the diocese would be met while Roman Catholic leadership remained intact. Kenny was the first person to be made a bishop of the Diocese of Saint Augustine who was not brought in "from the outside."

Bishop Verot was an esteemed seminary professor when he was assigned to St. Augustine, while Bishop Moore had labored for years in Charleston as a dedicated parish priest. In Bishop Kenny, Florida Catholics had a leader who understood intimately the ins and outs of Catholicism on the Florida peninsula. He would need little time to "break-in" or study the lay of the land. Florida's new bishop was a man of wide experience in diocesan affairs who understood the peculiarities of Catholicism in Florida. He was aptly suited for his role as a spiritual leader because he was accustomed to standing first in his class since he was a young man.

St. Augustine's third bishop was born in Delhi, New York on October 14, 1853. He is the first Florida bishop born in the United States. It is possible that his father was a farmer, as Delhi was a small town located amid the fertile and rolling green hills of upstate New York where single-family farms were commonplace. In 1862, his parents, possibly on account of bad harvests, moved to Scranton, Pennsylvania, a region where Irish immigrants congregated to labor in the coal mines and on the railroads. As a young boy, William attended public schools in Scranton and "as a young lad, he entered the employ of the Scranton Republican, receiving $3.00 per week for his services as a press feeder." He was quickly promoted to pressman by age 16 and hired out by the Scranton Times, a newspaper still in publication today. Almost overnight, a bidding war ensued between the two Scranton newspapers for the astute Irish-American boy. Eventually, Kenny went back to work for the Republican, but this time at a rate of $14 per week, a small fortune in those days. Undoubtedly, Kenny could have stayed in the newspaper business and made a comfortable life for himself. Fortunately for Florida, the constant lure of a priestly vocation played upon his soul. With the money he saved up from his work at the newspaper, he entered seminary at the College of St. Bonaventure in Olean, New York.

The College of St. Bonaventure was only 13 years old when young William Kenny arrived there in 1872. Founded by the Franciscan friars at the request of the Bishop of the Diocese of Buffalo, the college prided itself on its philosophy faculty and dedication to serving the poor. Kenny sparkled at St. Bonaventure. He received his bachelor of arts degree in three years, and upon graduation he was awarded an honorary masters degree due to his perfect scores in academics. He was ordained to the diaconate by Bishop Tobias Mullen of Erie, Pennsylvania, in 1878. But to become a priest, he needed a bishop to act as a sponsor. Apparently, Kenny wanted to enter neither the Franciscans nor the Diocese of Scranton and was immediately recruited by Bishop Moore to come to St. Augustine and work in the mission fields of Florida. At that time he was one of only eight seminarians studying for the diocesan priesthood in Florida.

William John Kenny was ordained to the priesthood by Bishop John Moore on January 15, 1879 in the Cathedral of St. Augustine. He was the first priest to be ordained in the now historic building. Shortly after ordination, he was transferred to Palatka to administer

ABOVE: *William J. Kenny, Bishop of Saint Augustine, 1902-1913.*

St. Monica Parish. In 1884, Father Kenny was moved to Jacksonville and made pastor of the Church of the Immaculate Conception. While at Immaculate Conception, Kenny set himself apart as a financial whiz-kid. Within four years of his appointment, he took the struggling downtown Jacksonville parish from the shoals of bankruptcy to the safe harbor of financial solvency. With fortune favoring the bold, Kenny was not afraid of highlighting his fundraising skills to Bishop Moore, who always appreciated the art of ecclesiastical bookkeeping. "You will notice that there was an increase in receipts in 1886 and 1887," he wrote to Bishop Moore in 1888, noting that there had been "an increase of fully $3,000 over the average annual receipts previous to my appointment as pastor."

Moore was impressed. In 1889, Moore named Kenny vicar general of the diocese, a position of authority second only to the bishop himself. Infinitely more impressive than his work with parish ledgers was his work with the poor and afflicted of Jacksonville. As mentioned earlier, 1887 was the year of the Yellow Fever epidemic. It was Father Kenny whom Bishop Moore relieved at Jacksonville when the Immaculate Conception pastor was attacked by the fever. With the help of Bishop Moore, Kenny soon recovered. Quickly, his sense of Christian charity thrust him into the hospital wards and fevered tent-communities of Jacksonville. Over the

course of the epidemic, Father Kenny energetically tended to all who needed him, regardless of race, color, or religion. A later summary of events indicated that "regardless of personal safety, Father Kenny was continually at the bedside of the sick and dying, administering the sacraments and comforting the afflicted." In fact, it was Father William Kenny's zeal and self-sacrifice that endeared him to all of Jacksonville. Indeed, his valor and efficiency would be remembered by city fathers only a few years later.

"With incredible speed the fire spread," The Florida Times-Union reporter hastily wrote on the morning of May 4 of 1901. Buildings in

ABOVE: *Early 20th-century gold and silver chalice richly worked with emerald inset from the treasury of the Cathedral-Basilica of St. Augustine.*

RIGHT: *Bishop Maurice Patrick Foley, born in Boston in 1867, came to the Diocese of Saint Augustine in 1896 as chaplain to the New York "Fightin' 69th" and 8th Michigan Regiments stationed at Fernandina Beach during the Spanish-American War. He was appointed rector of the Cathedral in 1903 and was named Bishop of Jaro, Philippine Islands in 1910.*

downtown Jacksonville "burned like cigar boxes, like chaff, as the thundering, mighty, lurid storm-wave of fire rolled to the east, ever to the east, and swept the area bare." Weary citizens and firefighters stood helpless as "at 4:30 a.m. the Catholic church of the Immaculate Conception, St. Joseph's Orphanage and the convent soon fell prey to the devourer." The Great Fire of 1901 was the single largest fire ever in the United States and would hold that distinction for another 23 years. Nearly 150 city blocks were devastated. The flames were spotted as far north as Savannah, while smoke was reported to have been seen in Raleigh, North Carolina.

In the wake of the conflagration, the spirit of the people swelled. With great speed, the leading men of the city formed a relief committee and geared up to rebuild the town. Rather than wallow in despair, Jacksonville residents determined to reconstruct their charred remains. Paramount among them was the 48-year-old pastor of Immaculate Conception Church, William John Kenny.

The morning after the fire, as smoke drifted through the air, Father Kenny gathered with the leading businessmen of Jacksonville in the Federal building and set about implementing relief measures. Father Kenny was appointed chairman of the Bureau of Information. Through Kenny's efforts, the local Western Union Telegraph station agreed to transmit messages to victims' families and loved ones free of charge. In addition to these responsibilities, Father Kenny assumed a leading position on the Emergency Relief Committee. This committee was

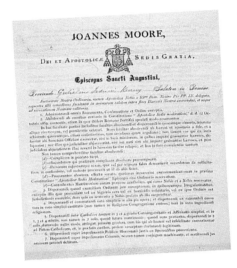

ABOVE: *An appointment letter from Bishop John Moore in 1880, granting priestly faculties to W. J. Kenny.*

BELOW: *Immaculate Conception Church after The Great Fire of May 3, 1901 which destroyed almost all of Jacksonville. The statue of the Virgin Mary above the entrance, however, survived.*

given the task of investigating and answering personal and written appeals for aid. Kenny took up these duties with energy and attention. All told, Kenny's committee received and reviewed more than 3,000 requests for emergency aid. Without a doubt, it was Kenny's deep sense of charity which led him to undertake positions on these crucial civic panels.

What is more important, Kenny's hands-on involvement in these works denoted a formerly unheard of Catholic involvement in civic affairs. Given the lingering suspicions of Catholicism which blew through the air in 1901, Father Kenny's leadership position seems remarkable. To appoint the local Roman Catholic priest to the chairmanship of a crucial emergency committee indicates that esteem and personal respect pushed religious prejudice aside as members of all faiths worked toward a common goal. It is not surprising, then, that one local reporter commenting on Kenny's installation as bishop in 1902 reported that, "not only in Jacksonville is Bishop Kenny esteemed and loved — the announcement of his appointment to the vacant See was hailed with joy all over the State."

Kenny's episcopacy was marked by efficient administration and a renewed effort to recruit seminarians from Ireland. Probably reflecting on his own recruitment by Bishop Moore 25 years earlier, Kenny vigorously marshaled young Irishmen from Mungret College in Limerick, Ireland and All Hallows College in Dublin. Both of these schools had traditionally prepared young men for priesthood in the mission fields. Future Florida bishops Michael Curley and Patrick Barry were both graduates of Mungret College. Even today, native Irish priests dot the landscape of the Diocese of Saint Augustine. Serving God faithfully in a new land, Irish pastors demonstrate Catholic Florida's "debt to Ireland," a debt which was happily compounded over and over again by Bishop Kenny.

UPPER RIGHT: *In 1919, Bishop William Kenny laid the cornerstone of St. Benedict the Moor Church, the first church for the exclusive use of African-Americans and the first African-American Catholic Church in St. Augustine. Previously, African-Americans worshipped from the east wing of the Cathedral.*

Bishop Kenny extended the work of his predecessors in other areas as well, most notable among them was his outreach to the former slaves of African descent. Kenny was adamant that the work started by Bishops Verot and Moore proceed apace. Most important, Kenny was concerned about education. Bishop Kenny took an active role in helping to rebuild St. Mary's Home and School, which attended to the needs and education of many of Jacksonville's African-Americans. Most of the African-American pupils at the school, in fact, were not even Catholic. Catholicism was neither forced nor expected, all that was required to attend was good behavior and a willingness to learn. With these building blocks, the Diocese of Saint Augustine cultivated a seedbed of educational promise out of which blossomed many of Florida's African-American civic leaders. But the capstone of Bishop Kenny's efforts in this area was his founding of St. Benedict the Moor Parish in St. Augustine, the first historically African-American church in all of Florida.

"Your appeal of Saturday offered to myself and my Council, shall we call it a temptation or an incentive to a Holy imprudence, was one which we could not resist." So wrote the "Millionaire Nun," Mother Katharine Drexel to Bishop Kenny in 1907. The daughter of the famous Philadelphia banker Francis M. Drexel, Katharine was deeply imbued with a sublime appreciation for the Real Presence in the Blessed Sacrament. She responded to a vocation at an early age. In 1891, Drexel founded her own order of nuns, the "Sisters of the Blessed Sacrament for Indians and Colored People." It was Drexel's wish that her devotion to the Eucharist might spur Catholic

TOP: *St. Benedict the Moor Catholic School was established in 1898 and in its first year of operation 90 pupils were enrolled. The Sisters of St. Joseph, who came to St. Augustine 30 years earlier to educate newly freed slaves, staffed the school in St. Augustine. Above are students of St. Benedicts with a member of the diocesan clergy, circa 1920s.*

missionary efforts for Native Americans and African-Americans in the United States. Of course, it also helped that she had inherited nearly $20 million from her father, a sum valued at close to one-half billion dollars in today's money. "Unless

something like the same sacrifices [of the Protestant churches] be made by Catholics," she wrote to Bishop Kenny, "in establishing Catholic missions, our Holy Mother the Church will claim only a few of these nine million [African-American] souls as her children." That having been said, the now Blessed Mother Drexel wrote her check for $1,200 and Bishop Kenny began work on building even more churches and schools for Florida's African-Americans. By 1912, the Diocese of Saint Augustine, in conjunction with the Sisters of St. Joseph, staffed seven schools dedicated to the education of African-American children.

UPPER RIGHT: *Mother Katharine Mary Drexel, known for her generosity to African-American people of the South, was beatified on Nov. 20, 1988 by Pope John Paul II.*

BELOW: *"A generation of Florida missionary priests," from left, Father P. J. Bresnahan, Bishop Kenny, and Fathers Henry Clavreul and James Veale, circa 1910.*

In late 1913, Bishop Kenny was still making gains in the African-American apostolate when he decided to take a trip north to visit old friends and drum up new donors for his educational efforts. Sadly, by the time he reached Baltimore he had become deathly ill. Cardinal Gibbons grieved for his friend and episcopal brother. Bishop Kenny's heart was stilled in Baltimore on October 24, 1913. As a symbol of his love and respect for his diocese, his remains were transported back to St. Augustine by train and interred at San Lorenzo Cemetery in St. Augustine. Florida Catholicism had lost one of its most revered leaders. Bishop Kenny was a man of foresight, clear thinking, and iron will. Yet, so often, as the diocese mourned the passing of great spiritual leaders, somehow new men were called to refresh and renew the initiatives of times past. Blessings shone on the faraway diocese. For even though Florida was considered an inconspicuous missionary outpost, it had the unique ability to nurture and attract men of impressive spiritual qualities as it bridged the future.

# Strength and Courage

## 1913 - 1921

*"A considerable number of Catholics have come into Fellsmore in the last few weeks. Yesterday, I held our first services in a plumber's shop, and I promised them Mass on the first Sunday of each month. Catholics are also moving into Vero and a number of Irish families have settled in Okeechobee. I was out there once, but at present the roads are impassable."*

— Father Gabriel Ruppert, OSB, pastor of St. Anastasia Parish, Fort Pierce, letter to Bishop Michael J. Curley, Jan. 4, 1914.

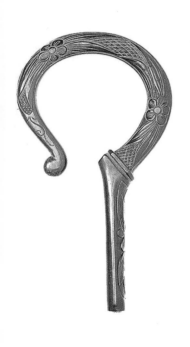

It was early April and the breeze was still a bit cool in central Florida. The local pastor of St. Peter's Church in DeLand was enjoying the end of the day tending to his orchard in back of the rectory. Clad in his overalls, he was conscientiously tying-up sprigs and pruning the branches of his beloved orange trees. A voice called from the rectory alerting him to a telephone call from St. Augustine. Somewhat reluctantly, he put down the pruning shears and headed for the house. It was Father James Greede, chancellor of the diocese. "Father Curley" Greede said nervously, "standby while I read a telegram which has just arrived at the chancery: His Holiness, Pope [now Saint] Pius X, 275th successor of Saint Peter, has deigned to appoint you Most Reverend of the Cathedral of St. Augustine." There was silence on the other end of the phone. Finally Greede broke in, "Father Curley, you have just been appointed Bishop of Saint Augustine."

He looked down at the mud flaking off his boots. "Bishop of Saint Augustine," he thought, "that is truly wonderful news!" Now instead of pruning his orchard trees in hopes of a fruitful season, he would have to play the role of shepherd, tending to a Catholic flock of more than 35,000 souls. He would take charge of a growing and colorful Catholic flock. In Miami and Key West new immigrations of Cuban Catholics dominated. In Tampa's Ybor City, Catholic Italian immigrants were setting up shop to work in a thriving cigar-making trade. In Pasco County, German farmers looked to the Benedictines of St. Leo Abbey for spiritual guidance. In North Florida, the great migration northward would upset the family structure of many African-American Catholic families. But even though the burdens would be many, it was clear that

ABOVE: *A crozier or pastoral staff used by bishops of Saint Augustine.*

LEFT: *A giant oak tree draped with Spanish Moss along the St. Johns River.*

Curley's brother priests believed in his spiritual leadership. They were certain that he would lead them to a fruitful harvest in the sun. But what was more remarkable than the constant support of his fellow priests, was that at age 34, Michael Joseph Curley was the youngest bishop in the United States and the second youngest bishop in the entire world. What was it about this simple country pastor that led him to a position of such serious responsibility at such a young age? While others raised their eyebrows at the appointment of one so young to a post so high, Michael Curley's closest friends and dearest family knew that Florida had received a gem from the Emerald Isle.

Michael J. Curley was born on October 12, 1879 in Athlone, Ireland. His house was perched upon the banks of the River Shannon, that winding and mystical river of Irish lore. The river and the rolling green countryside, speckled with ancient ruins of Catholic abbeys, allowed the 10 Curley children hours of healthy fun. The house was large and tastefully decorated. As young Michael rolled out of bed each morning, he could glance through his bedroom window and see and the gothic bell tower of St. Mary's Church only a quarter mile away. The church, with its towering sanctuary and massive colonnade, was an integral part of the Curley family's daily life.

It was in St. Mary's that Michael first served the Mass, learned to pray, and studied Catholic doctrine. By the time he was 14, he let his parents know that he would like to become a priest. Inwardly, his desire was to work in the foreign missions. As a young boy, Curley had been impressed by the life of Marist Father Pierre Marie Chanel, the first martyr of the South Pacific. Chanel had traveled from France to the Fiji Islands only to be slain at the hands of warring tribes. Young Michael Curley believed that traveling the seas to spread the faith was how he wanted to spend his life. At age 16 he traveled to the city of Limerick to enroll in the "Apostolic Section," or seminary course at Mungret College. The seminary was 75 miles from his home and administered by the Society of Jesus, the Jesuits. It was the first time he had ever traveled outside his hometown of Athlone.

During his first year at Mungret, Curley was ushered to the rector's office for a brief talk. "Bishop Moore," the rector told him, was "seeking priests for the Diocese of Saint Augustine in Florida." The rector of the college believed that there was "a great deal of good he could do in the fields of Florida." And so it was settled. Curley would finish out his days

ABOVE: *Bishop Michael J. Curley as a young parish priest.*

of training at Mungret and then become a seminarian for the Diocese of Saint Augustine, a diocese in a land he had never seen and in an American state of which he had never even heard. Deo Volente, he thought, "it is God's will."

Regardless of being away from family and friends for the first time, Curley excelled at Mungret. "He was an exceptionally conscientious and methodical student," one observer wrote, "possessed with rare powers of contemplation and blessed with a very retentive memory." On the playing fields of Mungret he was rated as a "solid, reliable man," particularly in soccer and cricket. His academic grades were such that the college sponsored him to take the examination of the Royal University of Ireland. The "Old Royal" as it was later called, was a diploma granted by a consortium of Irish universities for students nominated by their college to take the rigorous all-Ireland examination. Curley passed his examination and graduated from the Royal Irish University at Dublin in 1900.

The fact that he passed his exam is extraordinary in its own right. Popular wisdom was that the students from the Protestant-affiliated universities such as Trinity College and Queens College usually passed, while students from the Catholic colleges, which had little funding and regional faculties, more often than not, failed. At age 22, Michael Curley donned academic robes and took one of the finest Bachelor of Arts diplomas in the British Isles.

Next stop, Rome. Before he set out for the Diocese of Saint Augustine, Bishop Moore informed him that he was to enroll at the Urban College of the Propaganda Fide, the "College for the Spread of the Faith," in Rome, Italy. This college was specially suited to train men from all over

UPPER RIGHT: *St. Peter Catholic Church in Deland, Bishop Curley's first parish assignment as a newly ordained priest.*

ABOVE: *Father Curley's age at the time of his ordination as Saint Augustine's fourth bishop, created interest among local journalists.*

the world to be priests in the mission fields. It was also noted for accepting only men of exceptional ability. "I consider it my duty to inform you, Right Rev. Bishop," Curley wrote to Bishop Kenny in February of 1903, "that I received high marks in moral, dogma, and sacraments, with a 90 percent in Scripture." One of his new college friends was an Italian, John Bonzano, who was a junior faculty member. Immediately, the two struck up a friendship and made a running bet. If Curley would help Bonzano learn English, Bonzano in turn, would help Curley learn Italian. Over the next four years, the two spent hours together rehearsing their mother tongues and sharing in spirited conversation. Later in life, their careers would intersect in America.

However, all that studying needed to be alleviated by some relaxation. In 1903, Curley decided to spend "a most pleasant vacation at a villa high among the Alban Hills enjoying magnificent weather." In passing, he noted that he had the opportunity to "spend some very pleasant hours with Father Barry of Jacksonville," who was vacationing in Rome. "I certainly learned a lot from him about St. Augustine and the work down there." As yet, Curley had not even set a foot in the diocese to which he had dedicated his life.

Curley was ordained in Rome in 1904 by Pietro Cardinal Respighi, the pope's personal representative. Afterward, he sailed for Ireland where he celebrated his first Mass for his family and friends in Athlone. Then it was off to America. He reached New York and then traveled by train to Jacksonville in November of 1904. At Jacksonville he was told by the bishop that he had been appointed as the new pastor to St. Peter Church in DeLand, Florida. It was a long way from Tipperary. Now 25, as he unloaded his bags at the DeLand train depot it was as if he were in a different world. Small, rural, and with temperatures such as he had never experienced, DeLand offered Michael J. Curley a new challenge in his life. He got what he had asked for as a teenager, the opportunity to spread the Gospel message in a foreign land. His new parish extended 7,200 square miles, more than the size of the entire Archdiocese of Baltimore.

Right away, Curley made an impression on the local community. The Catholic population was sparse, but soon all of the Catholic families of

LEFT: *Father Michael Curley with his close friend Dr. A.H. McKewon, a benefactor of the mission at Rockledge, now St. Mary's Parish.*

BELOW: *Bishop Curley as a graduate of the Royal Irish University of Dublin.*

the area had welcomed him into their homes and hearts. These rugged Catholics were devout, poor, and hard-working. His first parish collection amounted to $2.25. Even so, he continued to make visits to the outskirts, conduct retreats, and offer excellent homilies. Over time, he became the "beloved pastor" of the church at DeLand, earning the esteem not only of Catholics, but of his Protestant brothers and sisters as well. He built churches at New Smyrna and a school for African-Americans at Fort Pierce. Often, he traveled the back roads of his parish teaching catechism and celebrating the Eucharist in Catholic homes. But if one thing came out of his DeLand experience, it was the conviction that ignorance of Roman Catholic doctrine could only be extinguished through the establishment of Catholic schools. Curley's commitment to Catholic schools never abated, and after he was elected to the episcopacy in 1913, it got even stronger. He needed to be strong, because by 1916, a new threat lay on the horizon — anti-Catholicism.

Easter Monday, 1916, can be counted as the "Black Monday" of Florida Catholic history. On that day, three Sisters of St. Joseph were arrested by the local sheriff for teaching African-American children in their convent school of St. Augustine. In early 1916, the Florida House of Representatives had passed a law banning white teachers from instructing African-American children. Since Roman Catholicism ignores race as a theological construct, the sisters naturally defied the law and kept right on teaching. Branded as criminals, these "nuns on the run" approached the judge and were eventually released under house arrest to their pastor, pending the outcome of a trial. When Bishop Curley heard the news of the arrest, he called it an "outrageous case," and vowed to fight it all the way to the Supreme Court. The spiritual welfare of Florida's African-Americans was at stake.

BELOW: *St. Mary Church in Rockledge, Fla. Built in 1917, it was the first mission church established by Bishop Curley.*

"It is in the ancient Mother Church of our country," Curley cried as he got set for battle, "that the bigots are now attacking and waging war in blind hatred and jealousy." "Michael J. Curley," the local newspapers reported, was "taking the defense for civil and religious liberty in the United States and the preservation to all the people of the priceless heritage of the Constitution." "Bigots are seeking to tear down the Constitution of our country!" Curley echoed as an adopted American. Without hesitation, he readied to bankroll the lengthy and expensive court battle which was sure to follow. Finally, after many days of heated argumentation, a Florida judge

declared the teaching law unconstitutional. But the nationwide notoriety of the case blew an ill wind through the state. In Tallahassee, one politician believed that he could win an election by running on a platform based solely on anti-Catholicism.

"The Florida Crackers [Florida's rural residents] have only three friends," Sidney J. Catts bellowed during his campaign for governor in 1916, "God Almighty, Sears Roebuck, and Sidney J. Catts!" Historian Michael Gannon has noticed that Catts' election as Governor of Florida was uncommon precisely because he was elected. Running on a platform of rabid anti-Catholicism coupled with a sympathy for the Klu Klux Klan, Catts steamed to victory on the heightened prejudices of Florida's non-Catholic majority.

While Catts warned of "Popish plots," and Catholic disloyalty, most Floridians sympathized even though they had never even seen a priest! At the time, Catholics were only three percent of the population, but suspicious Floridians were so riled up that threats of anti-Catholic toughs storming Sunday Mass became real. The feisty Irish missionary Father Patrick J. Bresnahan, in a somewhat obscured vision of Christian charity, kept a loaded revolver in his pulpit and stationed lookouts at the doors of his church. "Why did you tell so many lies about Catholics?," Bresnahan asked Catts after his election in November of 1916. "Brother," the beaming governor replied, "it was just politics." Thankfully for Florida's Catholics, it was not politics as usual.

Soon new forces taxed Bishop Curley's strength. American participation in World War I saw thousands of Florida's Catholic boys march off to the fields and trenches of Europe. Immediately, Bishop Curley set up a Diocesan Catholic War Council to coordinate pastoral efforts in the parishes. Parish War Councils sponsored prayer groups and counseled young men on Catholic sexual ethics before they headed out from their farms to foreign ports of call. Curley spoke at "Liberty Bond" rallies, raising money for the war effort and consoling the mothers of sons who had gone to war. Priests volunteered as chaplains and Catholic parishes, so recently under attack as unpatriotic, proudly displayed the American flag in the sanctuary. The Diocese of Saint Augustine, under Michael Joseph Curley's dauntless guidance, was

ABOVE: *Diocesan Priest Retreat, circa 1915, with Bishop Curley seated in the center of the middle row.*

coming of age. After 10 years of ministry, Bishop Curley had built more than 40 new churches, many schools, and Florida's first Catholic hospital. Consequently, his achievements did not go unnoticed by his peers.

On March 24, 1921, in Baltimore, James Cardinal Gibbons, the patriarch of the American church hierarchy, passed away after a short illness. Since his election as archbishop in 1877, he was the only church leader that two generations of Baltimore Catholics had known. And to be sure, Gibbons ranks as one of the greatest churchmen that America has ever known. But in 1921, since Baltimore was the first diocese in the nation, many observers expected an older man with a great deal of pastoral experience to be chosen as Gibbon's successor. That is why Americans and Floridians were shocked to hear that on August 10, 1921 the 42-year-old Michael Curley, Bishop of Saint Augustine, would become the new Archbishop of Baltimore. But should Americans have been so surprised? There to greet him when he stepped off the train at Union Station in Washington, D.C. was his smiling friend John Bonzano, who had been serving as the Apostolic Delegate, or Vatican Ambassador to the United States, for the previous nine years.

As Archbishop Curley took the reins in Baltimore, he continued to speak out for Catholic education, the advancement of African-Americans, and the dignity of missionary work.

During World War II, Curley would lead Baltimore's Catholics with the same amount of vigor as he had led Florida's Catholics during World War I. Certainly, his time in Florida proved an able training ground for later life. But as well-wishers waved goodbye to Bishop Curley, a new successor was needed in St. Augustine. The diocese was caught unprepared for Curley's rise in the church. The Catholics of Florida looked around them and after much introspection a suitable candidate was found from within their midst. Their choice was an amiable and beloved pastor who had served most of his priestly career in Jacksonville and St. Augustine. He, too, was a gift of Erin.

BELOW: *Procession of clergy for Archbishop-elect Michael Curley's farewell Mass at the Cathedral in St. Augustine, 1921.*

# Priest and Bishop

## 1 9 2 2 - 1 9 4 0

*"Catholics stood by the cradle of the American republic. They fought to establish this republic, and they have freely given their lives in defense of its liberties. We have no apologies to make for our profession of faith. We were the first to colonize this country, we were the first to land on the shores of the state of Florida, and we still keep the lamp of Faith burning in old St. Augustine."*

— Bishop Patrick Barry, excerpt from the commencement address given at Holy Name Academy, Tampa in 1922.

A ll the years of my priesthood have been spent in the missions of Florida," Bishop Patrick Barry wrote to Archbishop John Bonzano in Washington, D.C., shortly after his consecration as the fifth bishop of Saint Augustine in 1922. "For twenty-six years past, I have watched the growth of our holy religion and I am pleased to inform your excellency of the splendid development and fruitful harvest of souls resulting from the grace of God and the zealous labors of our self-sacrificing missionaries." To be sure, Patrick Joseph Barry was cast from the same mold as Florida's first missionary priests. "May God direct me and strengthen me to do His work in this distant portion of the Vineyard," he closed, not letting on that as an Irishman, Florida was doubly distant from his honored ancestral home. But that had never been an issue for Patrick Barry. As a young seminarian he had accepted an invitation by Bishop John Moore to leave his family and make the Diocese of Saint Augustine his new home. A home where he would live happily, labor constantly, and grow to love abundantly.

Patrick Barry was born in 1868 in the town of Inagh, near Ennis, in County Clare, Ireland. Nestled on the West Coast of Ireland between the Atlantic Ocean and the Shannon River, County Clare offered many sights of beauty and natural wonder. The fields and the seaside afforded the 18 Barry children a varied environment in which to grow up. With the encouragement of the pastor at Inagh, Father Denis O'Dea, Barry was taught Latin and Greek in special tutoring sessions which sped him on his way to the priesthood. As a teenager, Barry evidenced a religious bent and soon made it known to his parents that he would like to become a priest.

GENTIUM CUSTOS DEUS

ABOVE: *Coat of Arms for Bishop Barry.*

LEFT: *Father P.J. McGill outside Our Lady of la Leche Chapel located on the grounds of Mission Nombre de Dios, St. Augustine, circa 1935*

The natural choice for seminary was Mungret Jesuit College in Limerick. At the age of 19, he waved goodbye to family and friends and entered the "Apostolic" section at Mungret College. Soon, he began offering tutoring sessions in Latin and was placed in charge of the study hall. However, many at Mungret remembered him in another way, Barry was the only seminarian to ever catch a fish out of the River Shannon with his bare hands.

It was in the lecture halls of Mungret that Bishop John Moore, on a recruiting trip from Florida, first laid eyes on Barry and asked him to become a priest of the Diocese of Saint Augustine. Barry gladly accepted. And he would not be the last member of his family to head off for America. In fact, 11 of Barry's 18 brothers and sisters eventually emigrated to America. One brother, William, would also become a priest of the Diocese of Saint Augustine. A sister would become head of the Adrian Dominican Sisters and found Barry College (now Barry University of Miami) in 1940. Three Barry brothers would eventually graduate from the University of Notre Dame.

Barry, by nature, was easygoing but serious about his religion, potential life's work, and seminary training. Distinguishing himself at Mungret, he, like Michael Curley before him, also took the national examination and was awarded a degree from the Royal University in Dublin. But instead of heading to Rome for further study, Barry stayed in Ireland. He studied graduate level theology at Carlow College and was ordained there in 1895. Soon it was off to Florida to enlist as a curate in Bishop Moore's fledgling diocese. "Poor lad," it was said in the hushed halls of Carlow College as Barry picked up his bags, "he is going into the swamplands of Florida." Contrary to the naysayers, Barry arrived at the Jacksonville Railroad Terminal in 1895 relishing his new challenge and ready to do anything that the kindly Bishop Moore had planned for him. He was not yet 30, but he was wise, athletic, and eager.

As he stepped off the train, he looked around downtown Jacksonville and began to head for the spires of the Church of the Immaculate Conception, where he would become assistant pastor. As he knocked on the door of the rectory, he was greeted by a fellow Irishman with a twinkle in his eye. It was Father Michael Maher, whose lilting Irish brogue, put Barry at ease in his new faraway home. After cordialities

ABOVE: *Bishop Patrick Barry as a young parish priest.*

were exchanged, Father Maher indicated that most of Barry's duties would include teaching catechism, visiting the sick, and attending to the outlying mission at Mayport. That was what Barry had signed up to do. Finally, he would be sent into the rural "mission fields" to spread the Gospel.

In 1895 Mayport was a small fishing village, but was the most prosperous of all the missions in Northeast Florida, serving more than 50 families. There was a small wooden chapel there and considerable debt. Father Barry eventually paid off the debt, relying on the good faith of one of the chapel's elder members. From the beginning, he gained a reputation of paying off debts in a timely and efficient manner — a practice which would serve him well later as a bishop. Arriving at Mayport via bicycle, Father Barry would hear confessions until noon and then say Mass, sometimes an outdoor Mass in the fields. After a catechism class in the afternoon he visited with families until after dinner. Then, at the end of the day, the tired Irishman would go back to the wooden chapel. He set up a small cot in the sacristy and dozed off to sleep, close to the Real Presence of the Eucharist in the tabernacle and equally close to the hearts of his flock.

The Mayport mission and his duties at Immaculate Conception Church were soon cut short by a new assignment. This time Father Barry was to head to Palatka on the St. Johns River to become the rector of St. Monica Parish. The parish was poor and rural. The little town had never seen the likes of an Irish Catholic priest, but soon Father Barry, or "Father Pat," became a welcome addition to the town. In 1903, he built a parish elementary school. Because of his high learning and excellent teaching skills, many non-Catholic families in Palatka began to send their children to St. Monica's school. He was welcomed by the Mayor of Palatka and even the local Protestant ministers struck up a friendship with the pastor of "the church across the way." But while St. Monica's prospered, Father Barry's talents were needed elsewhere in the diocese.

By 1913, the newly consecrated Bishop Michael J. Curley called on Father Barry to found a new church in south Jacksonville. The Church of the Assumption of Our Lady was founded on September 17, 1913 by Father Barry and 140 Jacksonville Catholics. Within six months, Father Barry had the parish financially solvent, expanding, and ready to build a church hall. "Within three years," one observer has written, "all debts were paid off, the church beautifully frescoed, side altars added, and a fund open for a school building." By the time Barry's pastorate was up, "the Knights of Columbus had a flourishing council of ninety-seven members, the

ABOVE: *Bishop Patrick Barry's sister, Mother Mary Gerald Barry of the Dominican Order founded Barry College in Miami, now named Barry University.*

Children of Mary numbered forty, and the Altar Society, composed all of elderly ladies, was doing wonderful work." In October of 1917, Barry was called by Bishop Curley to become rector of the Cathedral in St. Augustine and Vicar General of the diocese, an office which carries the power of the bishop when the bishop is away from the diocese. These new assignments prepared Father Barry well for his call to the episcopacy in 1921.

"The population of Florida is being increased very rapidly," Bishop Barry's friend William Phelan wrote in 1925, "1500 families have moved into Miami in the last thirty days alone." "I was more surprised to meet names like Murphy, Hennessy, Ryan, and numerous others who should be of our faith but are otherwise," he impetuously wrote wondering how the new bishop planned to meet the growing need for new parishes. As was his way, Bishop Barry responded quickly and vigorously to the new challenge. In fact, he would build 28 new churches in Florida by the end of his episcopacy. He would also build 10 new schools and bolster the role of religious sisters in the diocese. Even more impressive, he increased the number of priests serving in the diocese from 29 to 72. But these moves were done quietly and were almost indiscernible over the long haul. It was Bishop Barry's concern for his fellow Floridians, regardless of religion, that garnered respect in times of social crisis.

In 1926, the winds of change blew hard against the diocese. On the evening of September 18, 1926, an unexpected hurricane packing winds of more than 150 miles an hour swept destruction and death over South Florida. Nearly 400 residents from Miami to Fort Lauderdale were killed. "After the storm passed nothing could be seen but wreck and ruin...lives have been lost, some by drowning, others by falling material, and a goodly number buried in the ruins of their homes," Bishop Barry wrote privately about two weeks after the storm. With optimism grounded in faith he announced, "Our determined people are girding themselves for the effort of their lives

*ABOVE: A picturesque view of marshland from the top of the Mayport lighthouse, 1922. In the center of the photo is the original St. John chapel.*

to restore their homes, their schools, their churches and public institutions. With God's help they shall not fail." It was Bishop Barry who, with God's help, took a leading role in providing relief. On September 22, Bishop Barry ordered all the priests in the diocese to take up a special collection for the homeless, those without food and shelter, and "the injured who require careful nursing and medical attention." Barry was convinced that the efforts of Catholics could help make the state "a fairer Florida than ever before."

As the diocese and state recouped from natural disaster, more looming yet subtle devastation was about to blow through the country. In October of 1929 the American stock market plummeted and dropped the country into an economic tailspin that would come to be known simply as the "Great Depression." Consumer purchasing crept to a standstill, personal savings evaporated, and creditors encountered sleepless nights worrying about repayment of debts. In the Diocese of Saint Augustine, Bishop Barry had taken out large loans for church building prior to the Depression. Florida was growing, the Catholic population was increasing, and the future had looked bright. Yet, after 1929, Barry would be continually burdened by the national financial crisis. But instead of allowing the diocese to sink into financial ruin, his management skills and financial prudence helped the church in Florida not only to survive, but even to expand. Barry's conscientious bookkeeping habits of years past now began to pay dividends.

Noting the "strength and sweetness" of his character, a major banking firm in St. Louis indicated to Bishop Barry prior to the crash, that they "would be glad to lend money, without any security whatsoever, and for a long enough time to enable you to comfortably repay it." And even as the Depression ground down the American economy, Bishop Barry's creditors were rosy in their assessment of his acumen. "Of all the Roman Catholic institutions with whom we have the honor of dealing — from Puget Sound to Bay Biscayne, from Chesapeake Bay to the Golden Gate, from St. Paul to Galveston" wrote William Bitting, Bishop Barry's mortgage banker, "there can be no doubt that the performance of the Diocese of St. Augustine has

ABOVE: *Father Patrick Barry as a parish priest at St. Monica Church in Palatka.*

BELOW: *A gathering of priests of the Diocese of Saint Augustine with Bishop Barry seated in the bottom row, third from the left.*

far and away exceeded that of any other one with whom we have come in contact, in your Divine Church." Surely, Bishop Patrick Barry was becoming an old hand at weathering storms of all kinds. "You have come through the burdens of leadership with courage and hopefulness — to the advantage of the church, your clergy, and your people," observed Father Edward Pace in 1932. Indeed, Bishop Barry had guided the Catholics of Florida through one of the worst economic disasters

of the modern age. And as the decades slowly changed, he would be asked again to lead his distant flock through even darker times.

In May of 1940, Bishop Barry was asked to deliver the commencement speech at Florida State College for Women (now Florida State University) in Tallahassee. It was a great honor for a Catholic Bishop to take the podium at a state university in the South, where Catholicism was a minority religion. "The Savior came nigh 2000 years ago and was called the Prince of Peace," he told his audience. "He preached peace and his last words before He ascended into heaven were words of peace — 'Peace be to you' — 'My peace I leave you, My Peace I give you, not as the world gives do I give unto you." Barry inspired the young collegians with words of peace as war dawned on Europe. These words, words of peace, were some of the last public words of his life.

ABOVE: *The Knights of Columbus at Gesu Catholic Church in Miami were among the first to establish an emergency relief station for the victims of a hurricane that hit Miami in 1926.*

LEFT: *Bishop Barry after delivering the commencement address to the class of 1940 at Florida State College for Women, now Florida State University.*

On August 12, 1940, the bishop walked into St. Vincent's Hospital complaining of feeling ill. The sister who attended as his nurse was Irish, from County Clare. It was a comfort to hear the lilt of her sweet Irish brogue; a homecoming of sorts. As the evening progressed, the bishop's condition worsened. Shortly after midnight, he uttered the name of his Savior and expired peacefully. "Laying

down the heavy burden of responsibility that had weighed on him for over eighteen years," one writer observed about his days as bishop, "this good and faithful servant entered into the kingdom of his Lord." Earlier that month, an acquaintance had asked him how many years Bishop Barry had been in Florida. "45 years," he smiled, and added, "one long, hot day!" However, Bishop Barry's "one long, hot day" had allowed the Catholics of Florida to face the challenges of the future with confidence and spiritual vitality. "Our religious tradition is a priceless heritage," he wrote not three days before he died, "It is ours to hand unimpaired to future generations."

Within days of Bishop Barry's death, news was sent to the mourning flock in St. Augustine that a new custodian of that priceless heritage had been chosen to succeed their beloved bishop. "Tidings of great joy have reached the clergy and faithful of Florida," the chancellor of the diocese announced on August 18. "Pope Pius XII has given us a new shepherd. Our Bishop-elect comes to us from the center of Catholicism, from the very heart of our Holy Father. He comes to us with the apostolic spirit and fruitful experience gained through many years of service to the Holy See." "Blessed is he who comes in the name of the Lord!," the announcement concluded with great expectation.

ABOVE: *Barry's episcopal gloves and zucchetto.*

RIGHT: *Portrait of Bishop Barry.*

# Patriot Bishop

## 1 9 4 0 - 1 9 6 7

*"There is a greater need now for a strong religious renewal to master the dangers of our American people going soft through prosperity. Prosperity calls for the strongest of moral fibers."*

— Archbishop Joseph P. Hurley, address to the Holy Name Convention, Tampa, 1965.

ABOVE: *Archbishop Hurley's Coat of Arms.*

LEFT: *Opening conclave of Vatican Council II at St. Peter's Basilica in Rome, 1962.*

It was August 16, 1940 in Rome, Italy. The clouds of war and destruction hung over Europe like a thick fog. Exactly two months earlier Nazi Panzer divisions swept south from Belgium and took Paris. France had fallen and all of Europe was embroiled in World War II. In his Vatican office overlooking the Janiculum Hill, an American Monsignor tapped out his latest letters to America on his typewriter. His name was Joseph Hurley and he had been stationed at the Vatican City State since 1934 as an official of the Holy See's diplomatic corps. From his perch overlooking the River Tiber he had encountered things that stateside Americans could only read about. He witnessed the rise of totalitarianism in Italy and the domination of Mussolini's fascist state. To the east, he watched warily as the maniacal Adolph Hitler rose to dictatorial heights in Germany. Now, as Italy declared war on the Allies and Hitler threatened to conquer all of Western Christian Civilization, all looked dismal if not hopeless. But just before he could slip into a state of melancholy about the world situation, he heard a knock on his door.

It was Carlo Cardinal Falconieri, the personal secretary of Pope Pius XII, and he had a message for the American Monsignor. "Joseph," the cardinal said after shaking hands, "as you know Bishop Barry of Florida has just passed away, and the Holy Father has it in mind to appoint you as the next Bishop of the Diocese of St. Augustine." Hurley was humbled — humbled to have been called to the rank of Bishop in the one church established by Jesus Christ. He accepted his new responsibility gracefully and Cardinal Falconieri left to arrange an audience for Bishop-elect Hurley with Pope Pius XII.

Immediately, Hurley rushed through the halls of the Vatican to find his dearest and closest friend, Giovani Montini, the future Pope Paul VI. "The Holy Father has nominated me to be the next bishop of Florida," he told the future pontiff, "What do you think?" Montini was excited for his friend and fellow diplomat. With his kind eyes he looked at Hurley and uttered a short phrase. "It is providentia!," he said in his endearing Italian way, "It is providence!" Providence is the direction by God of all things to their proper end. For Hurley, his posting to St. Augustine was the spiritual culmination of a life's work in the church.

Joseph Patrick Hurley was born on January 31 of 1894 in Cleveland, Ohio. With 10 other brothers and sisters, he grew up in hardship and austerity. His father's job as a steelworker and his mother's occupation as a laundress barely paid the household bills. As a boy, he attended the local Catholic grammar school and then moved on to Holy Name Catholic High School in Cleveland. Mainly because the family was so poor, Joseph ended up being the only one of the family to go on to college. Since he distinguished himself at Holy Name, he was admitted to Cleveland's Jesuit-run St. Ignatius College. Of course, the Hurley family could ill-afford to send a child to college, but Joseph so impressed his local pastor, Father James T. Carroll, that Carroll paid Hurley's entire tuition bill.

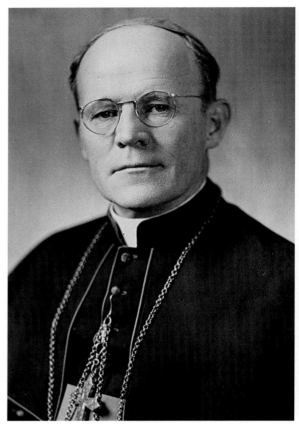

Drawn to prayer and the practice of his religion, he was made an officer of the college Rosary Club and excelled in his study of theology. He received excellent marks in philosophy and Latin as well. But rather than being a complete study bug, he took to the fields of athletic competition and had great fun playing collegiate basketball, baseball, and football. In football, he was known as "the breezer," or "breezy Hurley," since opposing tackles would only feel the breeze as he dashed by them toward the end zone. In 1909, his team won the Cleveland championship and Hurley was recognized as an "outstanding back" on a team that was undefeated. However, life wasn't just study and games. By the end of college, Hurley faced one of the deepest of life's decisions. He was torn between a secular life and the ongoing attraction to the priesthood.

He applied to the U.S. Military Academy at West Point, but turned it down. He toyed with attending law school at Harvard University, but never went through with the application. He wanted to become a priest. So, by September of 1919, he headed off to seminary for the Diocese of Cleveland. He found seminary life to be enriching and

ABOVE: *Joseph Patrick Hurley, Archbishop of Saint Augustine, 1940-1967.*

satisfying. He went through St. Bernard Seminary in Rochester, New York, and St. Mary Seminary in Cleveland with high marks and a cheerful spirit. In May of 1919, he was ordained to the priesthood, with his photograph proudly gracing the front page of the diocesan newspaper.

After his ordination, Hurley attended to parish duties in Cleveland. He enjoyed celebrating the Mass, visiting the sick, conferring the sacraments and helping the poor. Yet, after seven years of service at parishes in the diocese, providence moved again in his life and, like a bolt out of the blue, he was ushered into a new and exciting career. For many years, he had been keeping in touch with Father Edward Mooney, his former theology professor at St. Mary Seminary in Cleveland. In 1926, Mooney was appointed Apostolic Delegate (a sort of proto-ambassador) to India, the first American ever to represent the Vatican abroad. Hurley would accompany Mooney to India and, in 1931, to Japan when Mooney was appointed Apostolic Delegate there. In 1933, Hurley was placed in charge of the delegation as charge de affaires. During all these travels Hurley was exposed to new cultures, beautiful country vistas, world-class cities, and high diplomatic culture. These were exciting times for a young man who grew up in a grimy neighborhood in Cleveland, Ohio.

In 1934, Hurley was sent to Rome to work in the American section of the Secretariat of State, the Vatican's diplomatic corps. While in Rome, he was responsible for American church-state relations and monitoring political events. He attended to his job with flair and efficiency. Over his many years in the service of the pope, he had helped to smooth-over a host of diplomatic crises in both Japan and in America. Now, as a reward for his sacrifices and as an acknowledgment of his spiritual leadership, the pope appointed him to be the sixth bishop of the Diocese of Saint Augustine. As a Clevelander, his new episcopal see was as foreign to him as some of the plateaus he had visited in India. Exactly where was St. Augustine? He glanced at a map and circled the spot where he would make his new home.

As a mark of loyalty and honor, Bishop Hurley was consecrated in Rome on October 6, 1940 by Luigi Cardinal Maglione, the Secretary

UPPER RIGHT: *The consecration of Bishop Joseph P. Hurley as the sixth bishop of Saint Augustine, Oct. 6, 1940. Luigi Cardinal Maglione, Papal Secretary of State, left, attended the ceremony that took place at the College of Propaganda Fide chapel.*

ABOVE: *Vatican Diplomatic Passport of Father Hurley as Secretariate of State for the Holy See in 1940.*

of State of the Holy See. He sailed for New York the next week and after visiting his mother in Cleveland, Hurley boarded a train going south to Jacksonville and then to St. Augustine. We can only wonder what the bishop thought as the train carriage clanked over the Georgia border and entered the Sunshine State. He was back home in America, but he may as well still been in a foreign land. He knew no one, and had never even seen an alligator. But for all that was foreign to him, he brought new ideas to the church in Florida. His first thought was to create a central administrative system based on what he had known at the Vatican. Immediately, he set up a

central filing system, commissioned a parish census, and had photos taken of all property owned by the diocese.

Soon, however, he would begin to mobilize the Catholics of Florida for war. America entered World War II about a year after Hurley arrived in St. Augustine. But Hurley had already seen war in Europe, and even more, he had viewed first hand the power of the German army. He realized that American Catholics needed to turn their attentions to fighting the rise of Nazism. On the national level, Bishop Hurley became the most outspoken Catholic opponent of Nazism in America. Arguing that Nazi Germany was "Enemy No. 1" of the American people, he took to the airwaves over CBS and NBC to alert Catholics to the scourge of Nazism. In addition, Bishop Hurley spoke out on behalf of the Jewish people long before others recognized the brutality of Hitler's "pogrom against the Jews." He believed that America was on the right side of a just war, and he believed wholeheartedly that his country could defeat the dictators of Europe.

On the home front during World War II he acted as a catalyst for spiritual renewal and patriotism. During World War II, Florida boomed and bloomed like no other time in its history. Servicemen by the thousands descended on the diocese to train on its beaches, fly over its airfields, and undertake maneuvers on its vast land. But

LEFT: *Archbishop Edward Mooney and Father Hurley at the Apostolic Delegation in Bangalore, India in 1929.*

ABOVE: *Papal Coat of Arms from the Order of St. Sylvester, a diplomatic honor given to Archbishop Hurley in 1950.*

while the influx of soldiers offered an opportunity for spiritual growth, it also offered new challenges to the largely missionary diocese. Now the notion of a "priest shortage" set into the Florida Catholic leadership. Servicemen from around the nation inundated the churches, stretching parish resources to the limit. "Crowds spilled out into the street after eleven o'clock Mass," one parishioner wrote to the pastor of Immaculate Conception Church, "the lines into the parish hall overflowed into the street." In Starke, a relatively small railroad town, St. Edward's Parish was brimming to capacity at all Masses, serving the men of Camp Blanding. And in addition to all the American men and women at arms, the diocese was presented with the delicate issue of attending to the spiritual needs of the German prisoners of war.

As the war in Europe heated up, captured Germans were placed in prison camps throughout Florida, with the priests of the diocese valiantly meeting the needs of the spiritual over the national. "We shall know what is meant by sweat, blood, and tears. That is war," Bishop Hurley wrote to his flock after the outbreak of World War II, "But we should also add a fourth term: prayer." With this prayerful attitude, Bishop Hurley and the priests of the diocese led the People of God in Florida through one of the greatest challenges ever faced by the nation.

After the war, Hurley was called back to diplomatic service by the Vatican and appointed the Regent *ad interim* of the Holy See's Apostolic Nunciature in Belgrade, Yugoslavia. While in Belgrade, Hurley defended the interests of the Catholic Church against the persecutions of Marshall Josip Broz Tito's Communist dictatorship. In Yugoslavia, Hurley entered into a "savage battle of wills" with a

ABOVE: *Parishioners serving refreshments to sailors at the Cathedral Lyceum in St. Augustine during WWII.*

RIGHT: *U.S. troops gathered outside of Sacred Heart Catholic Church, Tampa in 1942, as they readied themselves for war.*

modern Communist who would have thoroughly destroyed all institutions of Catholicism in Yugoslavia were it not for Hurley's deft diplomacy. For his efforts, Pope Pius XII gave him the title of Archbishop and personally bestowed on him the rank of Papal Knight. Archbishop Hurley returned from Belgrade in 1950 and immediately set his mind to building-up the church in Florida.

"I am convinced," Hurley said to one of his priests, "that as Catholic leaders we have the moral obligation to look at least ten years into the future." When Hurley looked into the future of the postwar church in Florida, he saw a sprawling Catholic community. He was convinced that those soldiers who had bivouacked and trained in Florida would someday head back to the Sunshine State for retirement, recreation, and even to raise their families. Hurley foresaw a Catholic "invasion" of the state, and, as modern conveniences such as air conditioning and pest control began to make life more livable in Florida, his prophecies began to come true. But Hurley did not sit tight and wait for the boom to hit. Instead, he capitalized on a new plan to purchase real estate in Florida, a plan which later was deemed not only prophetic, but providential.

After World War II, Hurley asked the Catholics of Florida to reach into their postwar pockets and help finance church-building on a grand scale. After two successful fundraising campaigns, Hurley systematically began to buy vast tracts of land. One example of his purchasing skill was to buy parcels of land nearby projected interchanges along the proposed Interstate 95 system. The highway had not even been built yet, but he was sure that the proposed plans would soon become a reality. Soon, parish churches began to dot the sides of highways across the state. And Hurley was right. In 1940, the diocese was home to about 70,000 Catholics statewide. By 1960, even after the newly created Diocese of Miami siphoned off half of the state's Catholics, the Diocese of Saint Augustine could count an incredible rise approaching 160,000 Catholics. Thanks to Bishop Hurley, these new Florida Catholics had some of the finest churches in which to worship, some of the most well-trained priests in America to lead them, and an even greater optimism by which to approach the future.

ABOVE: *Pilgrimages to Mission Nombre de Dios were customary during the Cold War era when there was great anxiety about atomic warfare and Communism. Above, Archbishop Hurley greets pilgrims.*

BELOW: *Bishop Joseph Hurley, in 1948, defiantly rises in respect of Archbishop Alojzije Stepinac, accused by Yugoslavian Communists of having collaborated with Nazis and fascists during World War II.*

**A**t the time of his death on August 4, 1998, 86-year-old Archbishop Thomas J. McDonough had been a bishop longer than any other living bishop in the United States.

Before serving as head of the Louisville Archdiocese from 1967 to 1981, Archbishop McDonough was bishop of the dioceses of Saint Augustine and Savannah, Ga.

He was named administrator of the diocese in November 1945 when Archbishop Joseph P. Hurley was appointed *regent ad interim* to the apostolic nunciature in Belgrade, Yugoslavia.

Pope Pius XII named him auxiliary bishop of Saint Augustine in March 1947 and at the time of his episcopal ordination on April 30, 1947, he was 35 years of age, the youngest member of the American Hierarchy.

RIGHT: *Archbishop Joseph Hurley poses with priests of the Diocese of Saint Augustine in front of St. Peter Basilica at the Vatican during Vatican Council II, 1962. Among them are Father Michael Williams and Msgr. James Heslin.*

Much of this optimism was brought about by the calling of the Second Vatican Council in 1962. "The worldwide goals of this Second General Council," the Archbishop wrote from Rome in 1962, "is the growth of personal holiness and the spread of the true faith among your neighbors." He described Vatican Council II as a "great Christian awakening," and worked quickly and diligently to see that the Council mandates were implemented in the diocese. Soon, the diocese was transformed by the council. The Mass in Latin was replaced with an English text, altars were turned around to face the people, and more lay people were brought into leadership positions within the church. Even the Cathedral received a magnificent renovation in 1965, to celebrate the 400th anniversary of the City of St. Augustine and to show a turn toward the future in diocesan affairs.

Certainly, Archbishop Hurley had led the diocese through some of the most dramatic social and theological shifts in its short history. Since he laid the cornerstone of late 20th-century Catholicism in Florida, his sudden death on October 30, 1967, shook the diocese with shock and surprise. For the majority of Catholics in Florida, Archbishop Hurley was the only Florida bishop they had known. Archbishop Luigi Riamondi, the Pope's Apostolic Delegate to the United States officiated at Hurley's funeral, signifying the dignity with which the Pope valued his service in the diplomatic corps.

As a sign of his love for Florida's "good ground" and his commitment to his native flock, Hurley was buried at San Lorenzo Cemetery in St. Augustine. His passing represented a passing of an era in the church where "churchmen" defined and projected the leadership and spiritual position of the church to the world. Now, as the Second Vatican Council came to fruition in the parishes, that period of church had ended.

# A Wealth of Experience

"In the two hundredth year of our national existence, we witness the right to life denied while the right to death is increasingly advocated. These conditions demand that all men and women of good will rise in concerted action to defend the right of each person to life, a right that is God-given, and therefore a right that is both inalienable and inviolable."

— Bishop Paul F. Tanner in an open letter to the diocese, January, 1976.

At 8 a.m. on February 21, 1968, the telephone of the Cathedral rectory rang before morning Mass. Monsignor Irvine Nugent, the administrator of the diocese since the death of Archbishop Hurley, picked up the phone. It was the Apostolic Delegate in Washington, D.C., Archbishop Luigi Riamondi, who had presided at Archbishop Hurley's funeral a few months before. He was calling to inform the Catholics of the Diocese of Saint Augustine that they could look forward to welcoming a new bishop as their spiritual leader. He was Bishop Paul Francis Tanner, and he came fresh from the nerve-center of Catholicity in the United States, the National Conference of Catholic Bishops. Clearly, the Diocese of Saint Augustine had once again plucked a loyal son from the bosom of the church. The rural Southern diocese was keeping pace with its uncanny luck in gaining exceptional men to lead as bishop. And, as Florida's population growth climbed upward, the energy of its new pastor would be taxed exponentially.

Paul Francis Tanner was born in Peoria, Illinois in 1905. As he played in Peoria, he knew that something greater than himself was calling him to follow Christ to the priesthood. As a teenager, he entered college at Marquette Academy, a Jesuit school in Milwaukee, Wisconsin. He was a happy Midwestern fellow. A working-class boy, educated in a working-class town. After graduation from Marquette Academy, he entered Marquette University, where he received a good dose of Catholic philosophy

ABOVE: *Bishop Paul F. Tanner's Coat of Arms.*

LEFT: *Bishop Paul Tanner washes the feet of Cathedral parishioners on Holy Thursday, April 11, 1968.*

DOING THE TRUTH IN LOVE

and theology. By his sophomore year, it was time to answer the call. Would it be the Jesuits and their 14-year course of study or the diocesan priesthood and direct ministry in the predominantly German parishes of Milwaukee?

The choice was easy enough. While he admired the members of the Society of Jesus, it was in the parish where he felt at home; a feeling which would stay with him all of his later years as a bishop. He entered Kenrick Seminary in Missouri for two years before heading to St. Francis Seminary in Milwaukee for advanced theology courses. St. Francis Seminary boasted an expansive campus along the coast of Lake Michigan. Tree-lined drives snaked the campus, while Gothic architecture marked the buildings as authentically Catholic. While at St. Francis, the future bishop was active in the seminary Drama Club and literary circle. He enjoyed playing basketball and walking along Lake Michigan in the frosty cold. Scholastically, he excelled in philosophy. Later in life, he would use his love for Western philosophy to enrich his work and writings for Catholic teenagers. On his ordination day, the 26-year-old priest looked forward to serving the Milwaukee archdiocese for many years.

In 1931, he was made assistant pastor at Immaculate Conception Church in Milwaukee while also teaching religion at Mercy High School. It was during this time that Father Tanner began to take a real interest in organizing sporting events for Catholic youth. "Paul," came the ominous voice of Archbishop Samuel Stritch over the phone early one evening in 1940. "I will be unable to give the keynote address at the annual Catholic Youth Congress in Cincinnati tomorrow morning. There's a late-night express flight from Milwaukee to Cincinnati tonight at 11:00 p.m., I'd like you to be on it." After a bit of grumbling and a renewed "I'd like you to be on it" by the Archbishop, Father Tanner hung up the phone and began packing his bags.

ABOVE: *Paul Francis Tanner, Bishop of Saint Augustine, 1968-1979.*

In short order, the young priest jetted across the Midwest, checked into his hotel, and ordered a pot of steaming coffee to his room. He pulled an "all-nighter," composing a speech which was to be delivered to more than 300 delegates, and one delegate in particular, Archbishop Amleto Cicognani, apostolic delegate of the Holy See to the United States. With the alertness that could only be supplied by caffeine and heartfelt dedication to his subject, Father Tanner delivered a flowing, poignant, and altogether masterful speech on the spiritual

merits of Catholic youth programs. The apostolic delegate was deeply impressed. In fact, he later wrote to Archbishop Stritch asking his permission to "steal" Father Tanner, bring him to Washington, and appoint him assistant director of the Catholic Youth Bureau of the National Catholic Welfare Conference. And so, Father Tanner's "late-night express" landed him a recommendation from the pope's representative and ultimately a job in the nation's capitol.

After World War II, he had so impressed the American bishops that they appointed him Assistant General Secretary of the National Catholic Welfare Conference, a position he held for 13 years. And, from 1958 to 1968, he held the position of General Secretary at the Bishop's Conference. In this post, Father Tanner met many dignitaries, visiting churchmen from around the world, and virtually all of the bishops of the United States.

In accepting his designation as Bishop of Saint Augustine, Tanner indicated that he wanted to become "like the bishop so beautifully described by Vatican II." He wanted to "stand in the midst of his people...be a good shepherd, and a father who excels in love and solicitude for all." Nevertheless, he wanted to stand united with his people, and from the very beginning of his episcopacy, Bishop Tanner stressed the role of the laity in the diocese.

The diocese was still trying to digest the many changes of the council, and Bishop Tanner believed strongly in his role as a teacher. With this in mind, he reached out to the lay members of the Catholic faith and called for leadership from the pews. "The laity share just as much as the religious, the priests, the bishops, and the pope," Tanner commented at his installation, "in the broad mission of the Church which is to bring Christ to every human being."

RIGHT: *Portrait of Bishop Tanner.*

ABOVE: *Father Tanner (front center) celebrates St. Patrick's Day 1940 with a group of Catholic businessmen in front of St. Mary's Convent and Hospital in Milwaukee.*

As such, Bishop Tanner, using his connections from his Washington days, brought some interesting people to the church in Florida. Early on in his episcopacy Bishop Tanner arranged for Archbishop Fulton J. Sheen to come to Jacksonville for an inspirational talk. Sheen's network televison show, The Catholic Hour, was wildly popular among Catholics and non-Catholics alike. Jacksonville Naval

Commander John McCain, who became a Senator from Arizona and a Presidential candidate, also addressed diocesan crowds.

Theologically, Bishop Tanner presided over the North Florida diocese during some ominous times. In 1973, the U.S. Supreme Court legalized abortion on demand. Bishop Tanner became one of the most outspoken opponents of abortion and grieved deeply for the nation and for the women who chose to abort their unborn children. In 1975, Bishop Tanner spearheaded a move to have the United States Congress adopt a "Human Life Amendment" to the U.S. Constitution. The move was politely rebuffed in Washington, but it underscored Tanner's unwavering allegiance to the sanctity of life and the moral teachings of his church. Moreover, the same treasured philosophy and theology led Tanner to publicly oppose the pernicious evil of artificial contraception and the rise in cohabitation before marriage. Bishop Tanner was a man deeply concerned about his flock and did not run away from the scene of a head-on collision when Catholicism contradicted the social mores. In the post-Vatican II world of North

Florida, the impact of the collision was about as forceful as anywhere else in the United States, but in Bishop Tanner, the diocese was gifted with a teacher and theologian of clear thinking.

As he expected, Florida outstretched its Catholic resources in many ways during his tenure. Dioceses were carved out of Orlando and St. Petersburg in 1968. In 1975, mainly at the behest of Bishop Tanner, the Diocese of Pensacola-Tallahassee was created on Florida's panhandle. Bishop Tanner undertook another historically significant act in Florida Catholic history in 1978, when he ordained Father James Boddie of Jacksonville to the priesthood. Father Boddie was the first African-American to be ordained to the diocesan priesthood in the history of

ABOVE: *Bishop Tanner called for an Eucharistic Congress in 1975. In front, Father R. Joseph James leads a procession of parish representatives at the Civic Auditorium in Jacksonville.*

LEFT: *Father Tanner, as General Secretary for the National Catholc Welfare Conference, visits St. Paul Orphanage and Hospital in 1958.*

the Catholic Church in Florida. Father Boddie of Jacksonville represented a whole generation of native diocesan men who entered seminary under Bishop Tanner. During his 11 year episcopacy, he ordained nearly 20 men to the priesthood.

After 10 years as bishop, and more than half of his adult life in service to the church, Bishop Tanner tendered his resignation to Pope John Paul II in April 1979. Bishop Tanner was 75, the mandatory age for retirement from episcopal service.

Looking back, Bishop Tanner stated that his entire priesthood and life as a bishop was centered in the Eucharist, whether it was in the Cathedral of St. Augustine or a mission church in the hinterlands. And it was true. Only the Eucharist could give him the strength to carry out his apostolic programs. In 1968, when asked whether his appointment to the Diocese of Saint Augustine had taken him by surprise, he confessed, "I was thinking about some other ways to spend my retirement." But Bishop Tanner not only responded to the call of the Apostles, he thrived in it.

The diocese made great gains under this one bishop who inspired so many to follow Christ's call. In fact, Bishop Tanner became intimately involved in choosing his successor. "What type of man do we need in St. Augustine?" he offered. "Do we need a man who is a great spiritual leader? A community member? Someone who has competence in dealing with temporal affairs?" "Of course," he indicated in one of his last public interviews. "We need a man of all of those qualities," he said. Later that year the Diocese of Saint Augustine had their man, a man of many qualities.

*ABOVE: Bishop Tanner during his 1968 installation address at the Cathedral in St. Augustine.*

*RIGHT: The Bishops of the Florida Province, from left, Rene H. Gracida, John J. Fitzpatrick, Paul F. Tanner, Edward A. McCarthy, Thomas J. Grady, and William D. Borders.*

# Entering the New Millennium

## 1979-PRESENT

*"I would like to state unhesitatingly and uncompromisingly that there is one principal priority that the Church of Saint Augustine must always have and keep ever more clearly in focus -- that priority is to proclaim Jesus Christ as Lord. Every other priority must spring from and be rooted in that proclamation."*

— Bishop John J. Snyder on the occasion of his Installation Mass, Dec. 5, 1979.

"Pope John Paul II has appointed Bishop John J. Snyder, auxiliary bishop and vicar general of Brooklyn, to be Bishop of Saint Augustine," was the announcement handed to the press in October of 1979. Bishop Snyder, who had never visited St. Augustine, and decided not even to look at a map to see where it was, gave great thanks to the Holy Father who appointed him and remained ever open to God's will working in his life. But there was one problem, he recalled, "How will I tell my mother?"

Now, this 53-year-old bishop had to heed the Gospel imperative to leave home, family, and friends for the service of God. Mrs. Katherine Snyder was elated at the election of John Paul II, but now she had to deal with the pope's influence on where her son would live. "Mom, Pope John Paul II has made me a bishop in Florida," the loving son told her. "Florida?," came the somewhat ambivalent response, "doesn't he know you have a mother!" But the pope knew that Mrs. Snyder's son captured "all of those qualities" that Bishop Tanner alluded to one year before.

Bishop John J. Snyder is described by those who know him as "a very special gift from Brooklyn." Born in Manhattan, Bishop Snyder attended parochial schools in Elmhurst and Flushing, New York. He attended Cathedral Seminary Prep School in Brooklyn and took his theological studies at Immaculate Conception Seminary, in Huntington, New York. Ordained in 1951, his first assignment was to St. Mel's Parish in Flushing where parishioners remembered him as a young boy.

ABOVE: *Bishop John J. Snyder's Coat of Arms.*

LEFT: *Bishop John J. Snyder greats Pope John Paul II during his visit to Baltimore in 1995.*

After serving at St. Mel's Parish for six years, in 1958, he was named personal secretary to Bishop Bryan J. McEntegart of Brooklyn, a role which he retained under Bishop Francis J. Mugavero in 1968. He was appointed auxiliary bishop of Brooklyn in 1972.

Those days in Brooklyn gave Bishop Snyder a sense of the "neighborhood church," and the active role that families play in developing spiritual lives. Enriched by a deep pastoral sense of ministry, Bishop Snyder brought these experiences and his expertise to Florida when he was installed Dec. 5, 1979.

"I believe that it is the responsibility of a bishop to preach the Gospel of Jesus in all its fullness and be faithful to the magisterium of the church," said Bishop Snyder at his installation address at the Cathedral-Basilica of St. Augustine, "but then, like Jesus, to reach out and minister to people where they are at, not where we might wish them to be." He also said, "I will measure the effectiveness of my leadership, by the ability and willingness of this local church to call forth, develop and utilize the gifts and talents not only of its priests and religious, but of all its people."

Adhering to this philosophy, Bishop Snyder began to revolutionize the church structure of the diocese. He began an "outreach," rooted in the baptismal call, to various sectors of the church in light of the Second Vatican Council.

Moreover, he would get to know his people by living in their midst. "I want to be out there among the people, I want to be present to them," Bishop Snyder stated up front. Indeed, he's become the bishop most present to the people in the Diocese of Saint Augustine since the days of Bishop Barry. In St. Augustine where he lives at the Cathedral-Basilica rectory, it's not unusual for townspeople to see him pumping his own gas. Throughout the diocese, he always makes himself available for conversation and photographs at special events. "I need to live with other people," he said, "to share the joys and hopes of my brother priests and of the people on an intimate, day-to-day level." As his love for the diocese grows, he is deeply connected to its priests, religious and people, all the while keeping a special place in his heart for a special group of men and women.

ABOVE: *John J. Snyder, Bishop of Saint Augustine, 1979 to present.*

"Disabled children," Bishop Snyder said early on in his episcopacy, "are the closest to the Lord of all His creatures. For me, working with persons with disabilities is one of the greatest blessings of my priestly ministry." So disabled people throughout the United States have become real partners with Bishop Snyder in his Christian and priestly ministry.

In 1980, he established the Ministry to Persons with Disabilities, which became a model for Catholic dioceses throughout the country. Besides offering spiritual and practical help to the disabled and their families, the office has sponsored many new initiatives that are not only popular, but spiritually refreshing for the participants. Summer camps for disabled children, such as "Camp I am Special" and "Camp Care" attract campers from around the country. The camps, however, are only a part of major program development undertaken by Bishop Snyder.

ABOVE: *Teenage volunteer Brooke Aldridge and her special buddy, Brooksanne Cummings at "Camp I Am Special," 1999 a summer camp program for disabled children.*

RIGHT: *Marching with abortion protesters, Bishop Snyder prays the rosary outside an abortion clinic in Jacksonville.*

Of course, the motivating factor behind Bishop Snyder's outreach to young people in need is the same for all of his initiatives. Bishop Snyder has integrated in his own life and diocesan ministries, the late Cardinal Joseph Bernardin's "consistent ethic of life." That is to say, that all life is sacred from the moment of conception to natural death, and shares the same dignity grounded in humanity's creation in the image and likeness of God.

The ethic proved particularly constructive during the 1990s, in the wake of Pope John Paul II's encyclical *Evangelium Vitae* (*The Gospel of Life*), and its application to Catholics. In his encyclical, the pope

said the death penalty was almost always unnecessary and always contrary to the Gospel of Life. Bishop Snyder seconded John Paul's admonition and began to speak out publicly against the death penalty. Since the majority of Catholics favor capital punishment, Bishop Snyder's words of life have not always met with favorable civic responses. Nonetheless, by his public opposition to the death penalty, Bishop Snyder is doing no more than his predecessors, particularly Bishops Verot, Curley, Hurley, and Tanner, in opposing state-sponsored programs antithetical to Catholic beliefs.

In the same vein, Bishop Snyder through Catholic Charities has been a strong advocate of prison reform and has supported the efforts of Kairos, Justice and Reconciliation Ministry and New Hope, a program that assists ex-offenders to successfully return to society.

The population of the sunbelt, and Florida in particular, continues to grow. During the first years of his episcopacy, Bishop Snyder established an administrative hub, the Catholic Center in Mandarin, for new programs and ministries to serve these growing numbers. The semi-circular building, completed in 1983, is architecturally significant in design and has at its center the Sacred Heart Chapel, symbolic of Christ's presence at the core of each diocesan ministry.

*TOP: An aerial view of the Catholic Center in Mandarin that is headquarters for many diocesan programs and ministries. The Catholic Center was dedicated in 1983.*

*ABOVE: Bishop Snyder serves a homeless man a hot lunch at St. Francis Soup Kitchen and Clothing Center located at Providence Center in downtown Jacksonville.*

Through diocesan programs and ministries, and his own example, Bishop Snyder has underscored his active allegiance to Catholic social teaching. One example is the renovation of the old Immaculate Conception School building in downtown Jacksonville and the creation of the Providence Center, a social services and ecumenical center. Bishop Snyder's concern for the poor and underprivileged is highlighted by the ascent of Catholic Charities, which is one of the largest providers of assistance to the poor in North Florida.

An advocate of ecumenical outreach and initiatives, Bishop Snyder is one of the co-founders of the Interfaith Council of Jacksonville. It is comprised of 22 denominations and faiths and is coordinated by the National Conference of Community & Justice, formerly known as the National Conference of Christians and Jews (NCCJ).

Internationally and nationally, Bishop Snyder demonstrates his concern for ecumenism. In 1987, he was awarded the Brotherhood Award by NCCJ. In 1991, Archbishop Rembert Weakland, the chair of the bishops' Committee on Ecumenism, asked Bishop Snyder to co-chair the Anglican-Roman Catholic Dialogue in the United States. As part of his new role, Bishop Snyder journeyed to England with both Catholic and Episcopal bishops to meet with Archbishop

BELOW: *From left: Christopher Baumann of NCCB, Episcopal Bishops Frank Terry of Spokane and Robert Shahan of Arizona, Bishop Snyder, Episcopal Bishops Edward Lee of Western Michigan, Frank Griswold of Chicago, Franklin Turner of Pennsylvania and Father David Perry, ecumenical officer of the Episcopal Church, on a pilgrimage to Canterbury, England and later Rome.*

George Carey, the head of the Anglican Church. From England, they traveled to Rome and met with Pope John Paul II. Reflecting on that meeting, Bishop Snyder said that, "All of us were deeply moved when the pope said to us, 'It is already a wonderful gift of God's grace that we concur in acknowledging that ecumenical relations are an essential requirement of our obedience to the Lord." Bishop Snyder added, "The power of that statement tells us clearly that the search for unity is not an option."

Active on committees of the National Conference of Catholic Bishops, Bishop Snyder has contributed to the development of programs that address: women in the church, liturgy, stewardship of the earth, the mentally retarded and the oversees relief agency, Catholic Relief Services.

ABOVE: *Bishop Snyder is known nationally for his committee work for the National Conference of Catholic Bishops seen here at one of their annual meetings.*

BELOW: *Joining local delegates at the National Black Catholic Congress, Bishop Snyder reaches out to African and Native American Catholics through a ministry he established in the early 1980s.*

From 1992 to 1995, as chair of the bishops' Committee on Women in Society and in the Church, Bishop Snyder was a leader in drafting *Strengthening the Bonds of Peace*, a pastoral reflection on the church's need to further the role of women within the church and to recognize and utilize the gifts and talents of women in the church.

Regardless of his national obligations, Bishop Snyder's heart is never far from the people and priests in the diocese.

When he came to the diocese in 1979 there were 63,000 Catholics. In the new millennium there are more than 132,000 Catholics, many of whom represent our rich cultural diversity. Many of the Catholics arriving in the diocese represent the "new immigrants" within American Catholicism. Indeed, these new Florida Catholics are gifts to the church. For example, Bishop Snyder recognizes and nourishes the cultural heritage of many of our diverse communities, including African-American, Filipino, Hispanic, Korean, Native American, and Vietnamese Catholics.

Other newcomers joining the diocesan family are those entering through the Rite of Christian Initiation for Adults (RCIA). For example, more than 700 people joined the Catholic Church in 1999 which is remarkable considering the size of the diocese. Over the past decade the number of new members sharing their gifts with their new parishes has consistently grown.

To meet the diverse needs of the diocese's growing population, Bishop Snyder has established eight new parishes and seven new Catholic elementary schools. Plans are being considered to build two new high schools, one in Jacksonville and one in Gainesville. For the first time in diocesan history there will be 10,000 students enrolled in its parochial schools.

Facilities and programs for the diocese's aging population have not been overlooked. Five residences have been built for seniors with limited income as well as the new All Saints Catholic Nursing Home and Rehabilitation Center in Jacksonville.

UPPER RIGHT: *Vietnamese Catholics along with other ethnic groups in the diocese are encouraged to celebrate their cultural diversity at Mass.*

In 1989, Bishop Snyder established Marywood Retreat and Spirituality Center, a campus complex for group retreats, conferences, and prayerful meditation. Many parish youth groups use Marywood's peaceful setting on the St. Johns River for spiritual development and renewal. Marywood is also the home of the diocesan Ministry Formation Program which has received its initial accreditation from the U.S. Catholic Conference.

The five-year-old training program expects to certify about 90 parish leaders by the end of the year 2000.

Bishop Snyder attributes the success and development of diocesan ministries and programs to the generosity of the faithful who have responded with their time, talent and treasure. Fifteen years ago, Bishop Snyder established a Stewardship Office which encourages and nurtures sacrificial giving. Christ the King Parish in Jacksonville took this message to heart and is now a nationally recognized parish model of sacrificial giving.

Remarkably, through all the building and upsurge in Catholic immigration, Bishop Snyder continues to reach out to people "where

they are at." Under his guidance, communications, Justice and Peace Commission, migrant farmworkers, and people suffering discrimination have received his personal commitment.

While some of these efforts 10 years ago may have been viewed by some with skepticism, Bishop Snyder calls forth the gifts of the laity. With his encouragement, lay leaders have launched programs for separated and divorced Catholics, people suffering from substance abuse, persons living with HIV and AIDS, victims of domestic violence, Catholic homosexuals and their families. All of these various ministries broke new ground in the diocese and brought the spirit of Jesus Christ to those who might otherwise have been discouraged in their Catholic faith.

And clearly, discouragement has never been a part of Bishop Snyder's vocabulary. He is rarely seen without a smile on his face. A holy, happy smile which can illuminate a room brighter than the Florida sun. It is this smile, and his Christ-centered outlook that lead the Diocese of Saint Augustine into the next millennium and *ad multos annos*.

When Augustin Verot, who later became bishop of Saint Augustine, looked out over the missionary territory of Florida nearly 145 years ago, there were three small parishes, three priests, seven mission chapels, no convents and probably fewer than 2,000 Catholics.

*We have much to be greatful for!*

UPPER RIGHT: *All Saints Catholic Nursing Home and Rehabilitation Center in Jacksonville.*

ABOVE: *On the occasion of Marywood's 10th Anniversary, Bishop John J. Snyder dedicated a Marian Shrine. The new shrine is shaded by Marywood's tall oaks and is just a short walk from the center fountain.*

# TABLE OF CONTENTS
## Parishes of the Diocese of Saint Augustine

*Sermon on the Mount depicted in a stained-glass window at Immaculate Conception Church, Jacksonville.*

# CATHEDRAL-BASILICA

## *of St. Augustine*

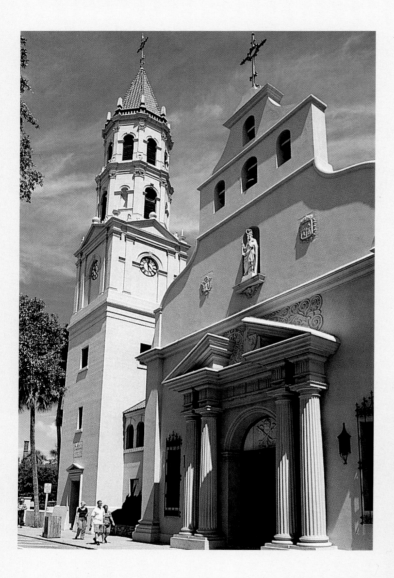

probably 50-by-100 feet, made of pine posts and thatched with cypress fronds. But in 1586, the church was razed and burned in the infamous raids of Sir Francis Drake, the soon-to-be English defender of the Spanish Armada. Through it all, Spanish Catholics held Mass in the Presidio, the local hospital, and the homes of Catholics.

Experiencing the challenges of cession and retrocession to England, a firm pastoral presence was not established until 1784, when the church took over the old "Bishop's House" property which is now Trinity Episcopal Church. In 1787, the small church was placed under the Diocese of St. Christopher of Havana. And by 1788, according to Bishop Cyril of Barcelona, "the Church of St. Augustine was progressing very satisfactorily" under the guidance of Irish priests, Fathers Thomas Hassett and Michael O'Reilly.

The church was administered from the Bishop's House until August of 1797, when the facade of the Spanish-style cathedral was formally dedicated. In 1887, the Moorish

*Saint Augustine, patron saint of the diocese, preaching to his flock.*

The Cathedral-Basilica of St. Augustine is the oldest parish of a permanent European settlement on the North American continent north of Mexico. On Sept. 8, 1565, four diocesan priests arrived at St. Augustine with the expedition of Don Pedro Menendez de Aviles. History records only one of the names of the four priests, Father Francisco Lopez de Mendoza Grajales and it is Father Lopez who began Mission Nombre de De Dios, where Mass and pastoral services have been offered every year since its founding. Immediately, a church was established and administered as a regular parish of the Diocese of Santiago de Cuba. According to archeological evidence from other mission sites in Florida, the church at St. Augustine was

*Blessed Virgin Mary Chapel*

building was burned in a great fire, but thanks to the earnest work of many parishioners, the church was reopened in 1888.

Architecturally, the church remained virtually intact up to a major renovation in 1965. At that time, Archbishop Joseph P. Hurley commissioned the building of a eucharistic chapel, the hanging of murals depicting the Catholic history of Florida by artist Hugo Ohlms, and the fashioning of a new tabernacle by the Gunning Company of Dublin, Ireland. Linking the building with the special care given it by its 18th-century Irish pastors, the newly renovated Cathedral was dedicated in 1965 by William Cardinal Conway, the primary cardinal of all Ireland.

In 1976, the edifice was raised to the dignity of a Minor Basilica by Pope Paul VI. As a testament to its historic national significance, the Cathedral was named a National Historic Landmark.

More than 2,800 families are registered at the parish of the Cathedral-Basilica. The parish provides many ministries and services including its Cathedral Parish School, established in 1916, where about 450 students are enrolled. Father D. Terrence Morgan is pastor.

# IMMACULATE CONCEPTION

## of St. Augustine

Established 1854

Long before there was a Catholic Church in Jacksonville, Catholic families gathered in their homes to celebrate Mass with priests who traveled on horseback from Georgia. This period extended from 1829 to 1854.

By 1854, Catholics moved from celebrating Mass in their homes to a small wooden building on the corner of Ocean and Duval streets. This was also the year that Pope Pius IX declared that the Immaculate Conception of the Blessed Virgin Mary was now an Article of Faith.

It was fitting, therefore, that the new wooden church building in Jacksonville be named in honor of the new Marian Dogma. In fact, William J. Hamilton, a priest from the Diocese of Savannah, was sent to Jacksonville to dedicate the church and become its spiritual leader. He exhibited a singular facility for ecumenism which so many of Immaculate

VERONICA WIPES THE FACE OF JESUS

Conception's pastors carried on through the years. Father Hamilton was, as one observer put it, "a man of amiable and social qualities that endeared him to all, irrespective of creed."

After 1857 when Florida was made a Vicariate Apostolic, "Cowford," as Jacksonville was known at that time, became part of the new Vicariate.

The 1860s were perilous times for the nascent church and for Jacksonville as a whole. In 1863, the town was occupied by Union troops as they prosecuted the "War Between the States." Sadly, some intolerant members of the bivouacked troops decided that the gates of hell shall prevail on the "beautiful little cottage" that Catholics were using as their church. The entire building was sacked, with Union soldiers marching through town wearing sacred vestments and blowing notes through organ pipes pulled from the church.

After the war, church officials requested reimbursement for damages by the U.S. government, but their demands fell on deaf ears. Regardless, the parish moved forward and established a school in 1868 under the direction of the Sisters of St. Joseph.

Fortune shone on Immaculate Conception Parish over the next 35 years as men such as Father John Kenny (later a bishop), Father Michael Maher, and Father James J. Meehan led the parish into its maturity as a religious cornerstone of downtown Jacksonville. Immaculate Conception was also the mother church of many of the first parishes which were established in the city's first suburbs. From 1881-1964 it operated a school that early in its history also included high school classes.

The present church edifice was dedicated in 1910 on the Feast of the Immaculate Conception. The former pastor, Bishop Kenny, presided at the dedication of the church which is constructed of white Kentucky limestone. Its interior is decorated with fine stained glass windows produced in Munich, Germany by the Mier Stained Glass Company. At the time Immaculate Conception was the tallest building in the city.

In modern times, "I.C.," under the leadership of its current pastor, Father Antonio Leon, has become the cornerstone of Jacksonville's Catholic community and has more than 530 registered families.

# ST. MICHAEL

**Established 1872**

## *Fernandina Beach*

Founded in 1872, St. Michael Parish in Fernandina Beach draws on a history much deeper than the date of its foundation. "Old Fernandina" was founded by Spanish explorers in 1632, but even prior to that date, Spanish missionaries from St. Augustine were venturing north to evangelize the native communities.

"The Church in Fernandina," the *Catholic Almanac* reported in 1879, "is dedicated to God, under the patronage of St. Michael, in remembrance of Father Michael de Aunon, who suffered martyrdom at the time of the Indian rebellion against the Catholic clergy in 1597."

Father John Bertazzi built the first structure in 1872 and in 1873 Bishop Augustin Verot confirmed the first class from St. Michael Church. Father John O'Boyle became the second pastor in 1879 and built the first rectory. In 1880, a group of Irish laborers began laying track for the Savannah, Florida, and Western Railway Company. The Irish-Catholics lived in a camp on the outskirts of Fernandina Beach. Like a pioneer priest, Father O'Boyle would travel to the camps, say Mass on a tree stump, hear confessions by the roadside, and attend to the other spiritual needs of his fellow Irishmen.

In 1882, Father Anthony J. Kilcoyne, a native of Scranton, Pennsylvania, became the third pastor of St. Michael's and the one who reached out most vigorously to the African-American community of Fernandina Beach. In 1886 he built St. Peter Claver Chapel that served about 26 Fernandina families. That same year, he invited the Sisters of St. Joseph to assist in opening a school.

Today, there is a monument in downtown Scranton dedicated to Father Kilcoyne, who "spent his days laboring in the Missions of Florida." One of the other early pastors of the quaint village church was Father Maurice Foley of St. Augustine, who later became the Bishop of the Philippines.

But even in the 1950s, the pastor, Father Joseph Ketter, was echoing the same sentiments of early St. Michael missionaries. "I sure have a rough time of it on Sundays," he wrote to a close friend, "saying Mass here in Fernandina at 7:30, then racing 26 miles to Callahan for 9:15 Mass, and then quickly back for a Mass in Fernandina. It keeps me stepping!"

St. Michael's has undergone several major renovations. The latest parish project, under the direction of Pastor Father Mark Waters, has been the reopening of its three-story brick school building, which had operated for 100 years

*Villalonga Family Cemetery*

from 1871 to 1971. It was refurbished and reopened as St. Michael's Academy for the 1999-2000 school year. Its renovation was embraced and supported by the parish and the school's preservation is also a source of pride in the Fernandina Beach community.

This northern-most parish in the diocese has a growing parish community of more than 1000 families.

*St. Michael Catholic Church Marian Shrine*

# ST. MONICA

## *Palatka*

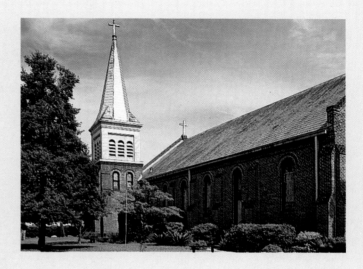

"St. Monica's Church on the St. Johns River," as 19th-century Catholics referred to it, remains one of the most pleasant spots in the entire diocese. Located in Palatka, the church was one of the many mission stations administered by the Georgia "horseback priests" of the 1850s. From its earliest years, the parish has served a lively mix of ethnic diversity. Consisting of Irish, German, and Spanish immigrants from St. Augustine, the church was ministered from Jacksonville by the plucky Father William Hamilton.

In 1858, Father Edmund Aubril blessed and dedicated the small wood-frame church. By 1861, with the advent of war, the poor mission church foundered in both attendance and administration since "the devoted clergy were away at war ministering to the stricken soldiers of the contending armies." After the Civil War, the mission was administered from St. Augustine by the hearty French missionaries Fathers Henry Clavreul and Joseph Hugon.

In 1876, Father Felix Ghione ministered in Palatka until the arrival of Father William J. Kenny in 1881. In Palatka, Father Kenny displayed the virtue and courage which would lead him to the episcopacy in later years. That same year, Father Kenny traveled to Tampa to care for a brother priest dying of the dreaded Yellow Fever. Three years later, as Father Kenny was called back to Immaculate Conception in Jacksonville, his spot was filled by Father Bernard O'Reilly.

In 1895, the number of parishioners, Father O'Reilly wrote, "were greatly reduced owing to the terrible freeze of 1894, which wiped out the orange industry on which the town mainly depended." Undaunted by the crisis, the little church by the river began to expand its operation and build for the future. On Oct. 31, 1897, Bishop John Moore blessed the cornerstone for a fine brick structure, which was completed May 4, 1899.

Father Patrick Barry, the eighth pastor of St. Monica, and in 1922 the fifth bishop of the Diocese of Saint Augustine, crossed the St. Johns River by small boat to minister to those in East Palatka, and then on horseback to those in San Mateo, Welaka and Crescent City.

The long tenure of Father William C. Becker covered 24 years and won the hearts of all the townspeople. When Father Becker celebrated his 50th anniversary of ordination in 1949, the town declared February 24 "Father Becker Day."

The church underwent extensive renovations in 1921 and almost 30 years later in 1950, Father Michael Kelly erected a parish hall.

In 1997, to celebrate the Centenary, Bishop John J. Snyder blessed and rededicated the church. Father Joseph F. Finlay, present pastor, launched a project to restore the church steeple and roof and other renovations. This whole project was made possible with a most generous donation by a parishioner, Mrs. Joyce Miller, who matched parish funds. Plans are underway to install a Carillon of Bells to celebrate and ring in the Jubilee year 2000. St. Monica Parish still boasts a rich ethnic diversity and has about 450 registered parishioners.

# ST. AMBROSE

**Established 1875**

*Elkton*

After having just arrived in Florida from France in 1860, Father Henry Clavreul writes: "Scarcely three months after my arrival, I was given the opportunity of exercising a part of my ministry in the Catholic settlement of Moccasin Branch, twelve miles south of St. Augustine." Such was the first Catholic outreach to the mission that would later become St. Ambrose Parish in Elkton. And St. Ambrose would, in time, establish its own missions in then-rural areas of St. Augustine. Today, these missions are Corpus Christi and San Sebastian parishes.

But back to St. Ambrose. The parish's namesake, Saint Ambrose IV, was instrumental in the conversion of Saint Augustine of Hippo, the patron saint of the diocese.

In 1871 the intrepid Father Stephen Langlade of Le Puy, France, set to work in the Catholic homes of the area. By 1875, the good father had marshaled his skills as a carpenter and the good will of his Catholic neighbors so that a small wooden church was built at "Moccasin Branch." The first Mass in the new church was celebrated on Feb.15, 1875. Ten years later, Pastor Langlade was celebrating Mass for a thriving community of more than 275 Catholics, including 94 children. His salary for the year was $103. And on top of his priestly duties, the rising number of Catholic school-age children necessitated the building of a school house in 1885.

"It depends on the weather," was Father Langlade's answer to Bishop Moore when he was asked how many children attended his weekly catechism classes. But certainly the adults were no "fair weather Catholics." By 1893 Father Langlade's parish had grown to more than 350 souls.

After the turn of the century, it was not uncommon to see Sunday caravans heading out to the mission for celebration of the Mass. By cart, wagon, and horseback they came. After the Mass, the families would spread colorful tablecloths under the majestic oaks and commence with a communal picnic which served as a giant Catholic community event. Children climbed the trees, men pitched horseshoes, and the women socialized.

Pastor Father Patrick Carroll, CSSp, has happily joined in the parish's long-standing tradition as host of the "Annual Fair." Hundreds turn out for this country fair which is usually on the Sunday before Palm Sunday. Father Carroll also ministers to the faithful at St. Ambrose's mission church, Our Lady of Good Counsel in Bakersville about 10 miles northeast of Elkton.

More than 175 families are registered at St. Ambrose.

# ST. JOSEPH

Established 1883

## *Mandarin*

Located 27 miles northwest of St. Augustine and 13 miles south of Jacksonville's city center, the small town of Mandarin was neatly situated to receive spiritual assistance from both the Cathedral in St. Augustine and Immaculate Conception in downtown Jacksonville. Since 1790, Cathedral Fathers Michael O'Reilly and Thomas Hassett ministered to the prominent Hartley and Plummer families.

In 1858, a small church was built and included a room for priests located off the sacristy. It wasn't until 1883, that the small rural community of Mandarin was considered large enough to staff a full-time priest or open a school. In 1883, the Sisters of St. Joseph opened a small school and soon after began boarding students in their convent, thus founding St. Joseph Academy.

By 1891, there were 88 students enrolled at the school, with nearly one-third of them African-American. That same year the families banded together and raised $48 from the sale of oranges and $75 from the parish fair. With their proceeds they bought Father Clavreul a new horse.

In 1921 a new church was built to replace the old building. It was in disrepair and no longer large enough to accommodate the increasing number of parishioners attending Mass on Sunday, a refrain diocesan officials would hear for years to come.

In 1971, the Buckman Bridge linked the fast-growing communities of Mandarin and Orange Park. A new parish school and gymnasium were built that year and in 1977 the "Old Church" became so crowded that Mass was held in the gym.

Nearly 10 years later, a new church was built to accommodate up to 800 families. But by 1990, Pastor Daniel Cody, found that the growth in Mandarin was outstripping even this newest church structure. In 1896, Father Clavreul reported to Bishop Moore that "the regular attendance at Sunday Mass may reach 100." In contrast, the average Sunday Mass attendance today has skyrocketed to more than 1,000 parishioners.

In April of 1999, a brand new church was built on what is now known as "Catholic Corners" and ranks as one of the largest churches in the diocese with 11,000 registered parishioners. And since the mid-1990s, St. Joseph's parish school has maintained an enrollment of about 600 students.

# ST. PATRICK

*Gainesville*

For decades prior to St. Patrick's establishment as a parish, Catholics in and around Gainesville received their spiritual direction from Florida missionary priests. As one elder parishioner noted, "During the war between the States, the Federals, or Yankees as we termed them, moved to Gainesville to begin work on the railroads." For many years, church records report that Mass was said at "Mrs. Young's Boarding House" on Main Street.

In 1886, Bishop John Moore purchased a lot on First Street from an African-American barber and authorized the building of a church. A short time later, the cornerstone was laid by Father P. J. Lynch, St. Patrick's first pastor. Father Lynch, an Irishman by birth, had a hand in naming the building after his native country's patron saint.

Within 10 years, the little church boasted 125 parishioners not including "a good many others who happened to be in hotels or visiting friends," Father Lynch reported to diocesan officials. In 1898, Father Lynch was happy to write that "the church is practically out of debt, with only a few outstanding bills of small denominations to be paid."

In 1919, Father John Francis Conoley was appointed pastor and immediately began to work with the 40 Catholic students who were enrolled at the University of Florida.

In 1950, Father William Balfe purchased property on 16th Avenue for the construction of a new church. And by 1959, the parish saw the need for a school. Father Thomas Gross built a parish school that was staffed by the Sisters of St. Joseph of St. Augustine.

In 1965, the Gainesville community continued to grow and construction was started on a new church. The old church was sold in 1970 and was later demolished.

Today, St. Patrick's houses the only Catholic school in the area. As an interparish school, it is supported by the surrounding parishes of Queen of Peace, Holy Faith, St. Augustine Church and Catholic Student Center and other area parishes.

Under the pastorate of Father Roland Julien, St. Patrick Parish nourishes the souls of more than 500 registered families.

# ST. JOHN THE BAPTIST

*Crescent City*

*The original St. John the Baptist Church. Today it serves as a chapel to the community of Crescent City.*

Florida "missions."

Through the 1910s and 1920s, priests came to town about once a month from St. Monica's in Palatka. It wasn't until 1932 that Mass was celebrated on a regular basis on Sundays.

From 1932 to 1959, Catholic growth continued in Crescent City. The original humble church of 1910, built for about 90 people, began to overflow with more than 200 parishioners. In 1959, Archbishop Joseph P. Hurley quickly purchased new land and approved Sunday Mass celebrations in the auditorium of the Women's Club of Crescent City until a new building could be built.

The new church and parish hall were dedicated in 1960. Fathers Burt Maher, Michael Kelly, Antonio Leon, Tom Sullivan and John Gillespie, among others, served as pastors respectively at St. John the Baptist Parish before Father Brian Eburn, the current pastor, was appointed in 1979.

In 1989 the dreams of elder parishioners were answered. The original church was renovated as a "beautiful little chapel." It was considered a gift from the parishioners of St. John the Baptist to the Crescent City community. A new parish hall was completed in 1990, signifying the growth of the parish in both numbers and spirit.

As we enter the new millennium, St. John the Baptist Parish has more than 525 registered Catholic families.

St. John the Baptist Parish was originally a mission church of St. Monica Parish in Palatka. Prior to 1906, Father Patrick Barry, later Bishop Barry, traveled to Crescent City to offer Mass only three or four times a year in private homes. With only a handful of Catholics living in the area and no passable roads, travel as well as communications were difficult.

By 1910, Father Barry and the parishioners of St. Monica's were able to save enough money to build a mission church in the Crescent City area. Small and wooden, the church was centrally located on Main Street. Church pews, land, and the Stations of the Cross were all purchased from the donations of wealthy Northern Catholics who were often pressed by their spiritual leaders to give generously to the

# ASSUMPTION

The Church of the Assumption of Our Lady was founded in 1913 by Father Patrick Barry, who later became the fifth bishop of the Diocese of Saint Augustine.

The parishioners had been renting a store front and priests from Immaculate Conception Parish celebrated Mass for them there. But when the congregation grew to about 150 people, the amiable Father Barry was sent by Bishop William J. Kenny to build a church.

Father Barry celebrated his first Mass at what was then called "South Jacksonville" on Sunday, October 5, 1913. A wealthy Catholic, William Byrne, supplied more than half the funds needed to build the new church; the Catholic Church Extension Society also helped.

By 1917, in addition to the fine church on Gary Street, the congregation also erected a parish hall and a spacious rectory. That same year, Father Barry was called to St. Augustine to become the Vicar General of the diocese and Father Patrick J. Bresnahan took over as pastor.

Prior to this assignment, Father Bresnahan had traveled the dusty back roads of Florida "saying Mass, catechizing, preaching, sleeping on benches, and helping to feed the ticks." He is counted among the famous of Florida's missionary priests.

Before Father Bresnahan left the parish in 1923, Assumption School was opened by the Sisters of St. Joseph with 110 students. And the school and parish continued to grow under Msgr. Malachy F. Monahan, who was replaced by Msgr. George Rockett in 1942.

In 1945, Msgr. Rockett began negotiations for the purchase of new land along the St. Johns River. In 1947, Father James B. Cloonan helped conclude the purchase of the property and he then presided over unprecedented growth in the area.

The thriving school was moved to the present location in 1949 and was staffed by the Dominican Sisters of Adrian, Michigan. The present church was dedicated in 1955 by Archbishop Joseph P. Hurley. The rectory and convent were constructed in 1956 and 1958 respectively.

A parish hall and an eight classroom building was added to the parish complex in 1965 under Msgr. Harold F. Jordan, who came to the parish in 1964.

Monsignor Eugene C. Kohls was appointed pastor in 1977. The parish now serves more than 1,000 families, with 625 students in the school, even though seven other parishes have been divided off of the original territory.

# ST. MARY

*Korona*

St. Mary's Church has a long and rich history based in the Polish tradition. In 1914, 35 Polish immigrant families arrived form Chicago to start a farming community near Korona. But by1926, it was clear that the wooded areas and climate made farming difficult. Many headed back to Illinois.

Meanwhile, a small steadfast community of Polish immigrants remained and continued to tend their beautiful wooden church. From the 1930s until 1954, St. Mary's was served by the Redemptorist Fathers from New Smyrna Beach. Since 1954 the community has been under the direction of the Diocese of St. Augustine. In 1989, the Catholic community in Korona celebrated their 75th anniversary. The mission community has built a new church and hall and the small church is often used for weddings and other special celebrations. The church, with about 360

families, is served by diocesan priests from Santa Maria del Mar Parish in Flagler Beach.

# OUR LADY OF THE ANGELS

*Jacksonville*

The Church of Our Lady of the Angels on Crystal Street in Jacksonville, a small parish by today's standards, is considered one of the pioneer parishes of the diocese. As early as 1912, a decidedly Catholic outreach was inaugurated by three notable women, Mrs. Henry Clark and Mrs. David Manner and Mrs. J. C. Miller, who worked with school children in the area. As their

children became more knowledgeable of their Catholic faith, the adults decided that they, too, needed spiritual guidance. Support grew and in 1915 a chapel was built and dedicated by Bishop Michael J. Curley. In 1917, Bishop Curley created Our Lady of the Angels Parish and assigned Father William Barry, as its first pastor.

Father John Murphy administered the parish during the difficult 1930s, with Father Michael Clasby taking over as pastor in 1940. But by 1943, with Father Clasby's health failing, Father Rowan Rastatter was named pastor and was responsible for retiring all of the parish debt by 1946. To celebrate, Father Rastatter was granted permission by Archbishop Joseph P. Hurley to sell Father Clasby's old 1935 Chevrolet Coach and buy a new Chevrolet Sedan DeLux. The Augustinian Fathers administered the parish from 1952 through 1978. In 1979, the parish was reverted back to diocesan ranks. At the same time, Father Joseph Notarpole was installed as pastor. Father Notarpole is the current pastor. About 80 families are registered at the parish.

# St. Pius V

The African-American Catholic heritage of North Florida owes a great debt to the parish community of St. Pius V, originally located at West State and Lee streets in Jacksonville.

There was a devout group of African-Americans who had attended Immaculate Conception Church since 1913. However, wartime race relations in 1916 soured. St. Pius Parish's history reports that African-Americans could not enjoy parish life to the fullest. "Seating was restricted to side doors, the youngsters were not allowed to serve at the altar nor were adults allowed to the sing in the choir."

By 1919, pressure for a separate parish community mounted. Similar experiences were felt by many faiths throughout the country. It was a watershed year in the sad history of race relations in America. The Great Migration of African-Americans to northern and mid-western cities depleted the South of its younger generation. In addition, race riots in Chicago and Detroit cast a pall over the entire country, including the South.

By 1919 Jacksonville's largest church, Immaculate Conception, seconded a plan to segregate its increasing African-American membership by building a separate parish.

On Sept. 14, 1919, Father M. L. Gumbleton, a Josephite priest from Baltimore, Md., celebrated Mass for 37 parishioners at Immaculate Conception School. A short time later, Mass was held at the Knights of Pythias Hall, a sign of even greater tension that existed among parishioners at Immaculate Conception due to the fact that the "Knights of Pythias" were known as a secret society.

Mass was celebrated in the hall for the next two years. On Feb. 27, 1921, St. Pius V Parish was officially established. Both the Catholic and non-Catholic community observed the event with much anticipation. As one parishioner wrote, "For it was the first time in the history of Jacksonville that the Rt. Rev. Michael J. Curley, Bishop of the Diocese of Saint Augustine, was called upon to dedicate a church for Catholic people of the Negro race." Clearly, while the circumstance of its foundation indicated sad divisions within the church, St. Pius V Parish blossomed over the years. Almost immediately, a parish school was started, financed by the Knights of Columbus, and enrolled 100 students.

By 1947, Father John Rottman of the Josephites had turned the parish into a happy and thriving spiritual community. "We have just completed a successful parish bazaar," Father Rottman wrote to Bishop Joseph P. Hurley, indicating that the parish had raised nearly $5,000, a huge sum in those days, and that new renovations would begin shortly.

By 1961, the parish community had outgrown its church building and on Oct.23 of that same year, a new building on Blue Street was dedicated by Archbishop Joseph P. Hurley.

Twenty years later, Bishop John J. Snyder dedicated a new St. Pius V Church in the presence of Father John Fillipelli, Superior General of the famed Josephite Fathers who had served the parish for more than 25 years. In 1994, Father James R. Boddie, the first African-American to be ordained for the Diocese of Saint Augustine, was appointed pastor. It was a double delight since Father Boddie is a beloved son of the parish and a tribute to the deep spirituality of the congregation.

About 375 families are registered members of St. Pius V; and its school, which has been operating since 1919, has an enrollment of about 190.

# HOLY ROSARY

*Jacksonville*

I n many of the early parishes in Jacksonville the establishment of parish communities came as a result of discernment on the part of local congregations.

In 1915, Dr. H.F. Van Trump called a special meeting in his home with other eminent Catholics to discuss the building of a Catholic church in the Springfield area of Jacksonville. Under the administration of Father Michael J. Curley, a small wooden chapel 45-feet long and 25-feet wide was built on the corner of West 16th Street and Springfield Boulevard.

The new church was originally designated a mission of Immaculate Conception and later Our Lady of the Angels Parish, under Father William Barry, shared the responsibility of administering to the mission community.

Holy Rosary was designated a parish in 1921 with work already underway for the construction of a larger church.

On March 4, 1923, more than 1,000 people attended as Bishop Patrick Barry laid the cornerstone of the new Holy Rosary Church. Father Denis A. Lyons was appointed its first pastor and celebrated the first Mass on Christmas Eve, 1923.

The new church was designed "on the lines of Romanesque architecture with a touch of the Gothic." In the niche over the front entrance was a sculpted replica of the "Holy Rosary Group," the original of which is in the Chapel of the Dominican Order in Rome.

A slate roof, bell tower, balcony, and pipe organ all were monuments to the devotion of the parishioners. The "Old Bungalow Chapel" became a Sunday school and meeting hall.

During the 1930s, a large Syrian community entered the parish and began to enrich the parish community. The Syrian Rite of the United States had about 900 members by 1942. In 1947, a major renovation was undertaken and a new organ installed. In 1958, Holy Rosary School was built on the corder of 41st Street and Brentwood Avenue to meet the growing pressure for education of parish children. The school opened with an enrollment of 344 children. The initial teaching staff included four Sisters of St. Joseph with Sister Mary Paul as principal.

The 1960s brought change and growth to the parish. This was signified by the arrival of the Redemptorist Fathers as Archbishop Joseph P. Hurley handed the administration of the parish to these capable ministers. Since promotion of devotion to the Blessed Virgin Mary was a part of Redemptorist spirituality from the time that St. Alphonsus di Ligouri founded the order in 1732, it was fitting that the priests welcomed their assignment to Holy Rosary. The first Redemptorist pastor was Father Walter J. Bueche, CSsR, who was given the task of building a new church for the growing parish. In 1964, a second church was built next to Holy Rosary School.

The Sisters of St. Joseph left Holy Rosary in June 1966. Ms. Jennie Pohorence succeeded Sister Mary Eucharia, SSJ as principal until September 1967 when four Sisters of Notre Dame of Toledo, Ohio arrived and Sister Mary Vernard, SND assumed leadership of the school. Currently, Sister Patricia Marie McClain, SND, principal and a team of dedicated sisters and teachers are committed to the quality Catholic education that has always characterized Holy Rosary School.

A new church was built and dedicated by Bishop John J. Snyder on Oct. 7, 1984. Currently there are about 225 registered families at Holy Rosary and Father Glenn D. Parker, CSsR maintains the Redemptorist spirit of the parish as its pastor.

# ST. PAUL

In 1885, Jacksonville's Riverside district registered only 370 people and was considered a "suburb" of the city. Just 38 years later in 1923, the Catholic population alone measured more than 1,000 souls. As happens often in church history, local "movements" stir church leaders to establish houses of worship. Such was the case with St. Paul Catholic Church in Riverside.

As early as 1914, a group of neighborhood Catholics convinced then Bishop Michael J. Curley to purchase a lot on the corner of Park and King Streets for about $12,000, a healthy sum in 1914. With the Catholic population growing and the "big" church, Immaculate Conception, too far away, Catholics living in Riverside banded together in founding a parish in 1922. That same year, it also became clear that the original property was inadequate and new land was purchased on Park and Acosta streets for a building that would house the church, school and an auditorium.

On Easter Sunday, 1923, Bishop Patrick Barry laid the cornerstone of St. Paul's Church and appointed his brother, Father William

Barry, its first pastor. Mass was celebrated for the first time in the church auditorium on Sept. 16, 1923.

In November, a convent was completed for the Sisters of St. Joseph and the former property located on Park Street was sold. Proceeds from the sale of the property were donated to the parish by Bishop Barry, but the convent, church, school, and the auditorium ultimately cost the fledgling parish about $100,000, an ominous sum with the Great Depression looming five years distant.

During the 1930s the parish kept its former growth pattern and, thanks to the financial savvy of Bishop Barry and Msgr. Denis Lyons, the new pastor, more land was purchased on Park Street for a new church building. Ground was broken in 1939 and the new church was completed in 1940. One of the first public acts in the Diocese of Saint Augustine by Bishop Joseph P. Hurley was confirmation at St. Paul.

Constructed of yellow brick with limestone trim, the church was considered an architectural gem for the area. In 1949, the esteemed Msgr. Patrick E. Nolan was appointed pastor and led the parish through the unsettled times of the 1960s and into the 1970s.

Father Michael J. Kelly became pastor in 1970 and he retired in 1983. Father Thomas Sullivan, who is currently the pastor, guided a good deal of educational reform at St. Paul's School. A Montessori pre-school and kindergarten were developed while a Special Education program was established for the grade school.

St. Paul's Riverside, which is in an area best known for the preservation and renovation of its beautiful old homes, serves more than 500 registered families.

# St. Augustine Church and Catholic Student Center

## Established 1923

## Gainesville

It was Father John F. Conoley, pastor of St. Patrick's in Gainesville, who first recognized the need for a Catholic student residence at the University of Florida in 1920. In 1923 a generous benefactor, Mary A. Crane of New York City, donated $40,000 to Father Conoley.

Shortly after Crane Hall was established as a residence for Catholic students. The red brick building was architecturally similar to the surrounding university buildings and housed a beautiful private chapel on the first floor. After this building was demolished in 1958, Mass was celebrated at Thomas House, now known as Hurley Hall. In 1959, Archbishop Joseph P. Hurley dedicated the Chapel of Saint Augustine and the Student Center was established as an independent parish community.

By the 1960s, the spirit of social justice, that has long characterized the charism of the parish, became more pronounced. As the war in Vietnam heated up, priests from the Student Center were some of the first to lead anti-war protests. Beginning in 1968, a semi-annual "Mass on the grass" was offered by Father Michael Gannon on the university's Plaza of the Americas.

In the late 1970's, following a tradition of openness and accessibility, Father Robert Baker, Pastor (now Bishop of Charleston, SC), established St. Francis House, a shelter and soup kitchen for the homeless.

In 1981, Father John D. Gillespie began his pastorate. He encouraged even greater lay participation, expanding programs to meet the needs of the present day. In addition, Father Gillespie began to take a deep interest in community issues, including community policies affecting the poor and marginalized.

Currently, there are nearly 10,000 Catholic students attending institutions of higher learning in Gainesville, and St. Augustine's has become the gathering place for their shared spiritual and intellectual experience. More than 500 families are registered at the parish.

*This statue, "Tolle et Lege", depicts the conversion of Saint Augustine and was dedicated to all students who labor prayerfully in pursuit of the truth. St. Augustine sculptor Enzo Torcoletti, crafted the statue which was dedicated on March 15, 1980.*

# SACRED HEART

## Green Cove Springs

In the early days of the diocese, Sacred Heart Church in Green Cove Springs was a mission of the Cathedral in St. Augustine. Over the years, future Bishops William J. Kenny and Patrick Barry both visited the small church to celebrate Easter Sunday Mass and to hear confessions.

The first church structure was built in 1874 by Philip J. Canova and his son Rafael. Priests visited the mission once or twice a month during the 1880s. The Cathedral Parish conducted a census in 1893 and 35 Catholics were identified as living in Green Cove Springs. Twenty years later, a new census recorded 61 Catholics in the territory.

By the time Father Patrick J. Bresnahan visited the mission church in the1930s he noticed that, "Like other places in the state, Green Cove Springs has increased in population, and naturally the Catholic contingent will increase in proportion." But even Father Bresnahan could not foretell the changes that the next decade would bring for the sleepy town of Green Cove Springs.

The first documented resident priest for Green Cove Springs was Father James P. Kerr, who also served the mission in Orange Park, now known as St. Catherine Parish, in 1940. During 1941, Thomas J. McDonough, a priest from Philadelphia who would later become the Auxiliary Bishop of the Diocese of Saint Augustine, was named pastor of Sacred Heart.

It was during the war years of the 1940s that the little country parish sprang into a worship place for Catholic men from around the globe. Almost overnight, the U.S. Naval and Coast Guard installations near Green Cove Springs started to tax the rural parish. The "new" Sacred Heart Church was dedicated after the war in June of 1954 by Thomas McDonough. "Upon my arrival in Florida the first parish assignment given me by Bishop Hurley was that of Administrator of the Church of the Sacred Heart,"

McDonough recalled as he dedicated the new building. "I cherish many happy memories from the days I spent in this parish," he added.

The first pastor of the new church was Father John W. Love, an altogether exemplary priest, administrator, and a man who was loved by his community. Eventually, Father Love was named Chancellor of the diocese, and his sudden death in 1950 brought much sorrow to the community of Sacred Heart.

The original church from 1947 still stands as a monument to the generosity and sacrifice of the Catholics of Green Cove Springs.

Father Donal Sullivan, who was appointed pastor in 1994, continues to lead the parish into the new century with an emphasis on Catholic education and meeting the growing needs of Catholics in Clay County. For example, In 1993, Sacred Heart became one of three parishes which founded and supports Annunciation School, an interparish elementary school in Middleburg.

Sacred Heart has more than 460 registered families. But those numbers are expected to increase, so the parish will be building a new church on Fleming Island and is expected to be completed in 2001.

# ST. PAUL

## Jacksonville Beach

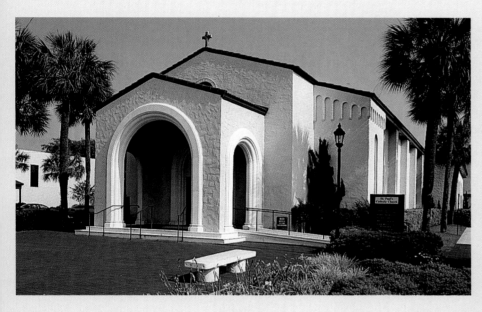

ince the 1830s circuit-riding missionaries from St. Augustine's Cathedral had been venturing up to "St. Johns Bar," as it was known then, to gather scattered Catholics in neighborhood homes for the celebration of the Eucharist.

When William J. Kenny was the only priest in Jacksonville, he appealed to the members of Immaculate Conception Church, the mother parish of Jacksonville, to lend financial assistance for the building of a chapel at "Pablo Beach." After the turn of the century, the Jacksonville area beach began to blossom as "Florida's great summer resort," and boasted "a peerless beach," for vacationing tourists.

In 1890, Father Kenny and Father Charles Mohr, OSB, of St. Leo Abbey near Tampa, dedicated a large bell to the memory of St. Paul and rang the Te Deum in celebration for the success of the parish. The small wooden chapel with the high bell tower was only used in summertime and was attended by Father Michael Maher of Jacksonville, and two future bishops of the diocese, Fathers William Kenney and Patrick Barry.

The little chapel at the beach fell under the jurisdiction of Assumption Parish in South Jacksonville and by 1921 Father Patrick J. Bresnahan was traveling to Pablo Beach on the first and third Sundays of the month to celebrate Mass. A resident pastor was appointed on July 6, 1923, when Bishop Patrick Barry named the resort a parish and appointed Father Dennis J. O'Keefe as its first resident

pastor. And since there was no rectory, "the pastor was making his headquarters at the Orphans Summer Resort."

In 1930, Father Cornelius J. Murphy was made pastor of a year-round Catholic community of only 35 people. By that time, the Great Depression intervened and precipitated some lean years for the beachside parish community. But by 1937, and mostly due to Bishop Barry's deft handling of financial accounts, an entire city block was purchased for future church development.

Four years later, Father Murphy was able to break ground for the present church. St. Paul School was opened in 1950 and enlarged in 1958 by Msgr. James J. Heslin. Father Diego Conesa was appointed pastor in 1969 and began making major renovations right away.

The church sanctuary was renovated and a cry room was added. In 1977, Father William A. Kelly was appointed pastor. In 1985, the school was renovated and enlarged with a parish center and gymnasium being added two years later. Over the years, St. Paul's has grown from a friendly community of believers gathering in homes along the seashore into a major parish with a thriving youth and young adult program. Through all the institutional changes, however, neither the devotion of the parishioners nor the cheerfulness of their spirit has diminished.

St. Paul Parish boasts more than 2,350 registered families. Its school, which has been in operation since 1950, has an enrollment of 560 students.

# ST. EDWARD

## *Starke*

The early years of Catholicism in and around Starke are obscure and undocumented. We know that in 1854 a Georgia farmer by the name of Drury Reddish obtained a 40-acre plot and named the area South Starke.

In 1857, Benjamin Frisbee and his wife Mary Ann donated the property where the current church is located "for the use and benefit of the Catholics." Toward the end of the 19th century, Father Edmund Clavreul intermittently visited Starke from his post at St. Michael Parish in Fernandina Beach, celebrating Mass, hearing confessions, and spiritually guiding the Catholic families there.

By 1860, Starke was "booming" as an active railroad terminus. During this period, the Catholics in Starke attended Mass either at Catholic homes in Gainesville or at Immaculate Conception Church in Jacksonville.

In March of 1872, Bishop Augustin Verot visited Starke and confirmed its Catholic children, one of whom was Edward Pace. He is the first son of Starke to enter the priesthood. Pace would later become the first American to hold a doctorate in psychology and taught on the faculty of The Catholic University of America for nearly 40 years.

As a seminarian in Rome, Pace was invited to engage in a student disputata, or philosophical debate, in front of his peers and teachers. The winner of the debate was to be judged by none other than Pope Leo XIII. For more than an hour, Pace wowed the audience with his knowledge and presentation of philosophy. His Holiness, Pope Leo, was so impressed with the thin redheaded boy from Starke that he immediately dispensed him from his doctoral examinations and awarded the young man his passing grade right then and there. And the legacy of Edward Pace is intimately tied to

the parish. On Oct.13, 1941, the parish church was dedicated to St. Edward the Confessor as the namesake of Father Edward Pace.

The founding pastor of St. Edward's was Father Thomas J. Murphy, who served until 1943 when he was replaced by Father Michael Fogarty. Of course, World War II brought many changes. With the expansion of nearby Camp Blanding, Catholics associated with the U.S. Army stretched the resources of the small parish.

In 1942, the U.S. government and the United Catholic Community Service Organization joined efforts in building a USO Club for the tiny parish. After the war, as penal institutions at Lawtey and Raiford were constructed, the pastoral mission of the parish became oriented to prison ministry as well.

Father William Hochheim, the current pastor, was installed as pastor of St. Edward's in 1989 and serves about 100 families.

# ST. MATTHEW

St. Matthew Parish, located on Blanding Boulevard in Jacksonville, owes a good deal of its history to the Army National Guard camp after which the street is named. In fact, the first church structure used for worship was the old military chapel at Camp Blanding.

In 1948, the Army chapel was deconstructed and moved in seven separate parts to Blanding Boulevard. The parish was founded on Nov. 14, 1947, but for two years the Catholics of the area celebrated Mass twice on Sunday in the Lake Shore Theater. Father Joseph Corde was assigned to organize the foundation of a parish community. He was an associate pastor at St. Paul Parish in the Riverside area of Jacksonville which is considered the mother parish of St. Matthew's. When the parish was founded, there were nearly 250 families registered in the parish.

"It's a nice new church," Father Corde recorded in a 1950 memorandum to the chancery, describing the new reconstructed Army chapel. By January of 1950 a parish hall was built and later it was connected to the parish school. In September of 1951 St. Matthew Parish School was built and opened for classes to about 200 students.

Principal Sister Helen Thomas and four other Adrian Dominican Sisters began teaching in the school. The parish flourished during the 1950s and by 1954 a new building campaign was initiated.

In December of 1956, a new brick church seating more than 800 people was built. By 1965, the school registered more than 400 students and nine teaching sisters.

Esteemed pastors of St. Matthew's include: Father Corde, Father Paul Leo Manning, Father Daniel C. Hegarty, and for a time, Father Thomas J. McDonough, who later became a bishop, and Msgr. John Burns. Msgr. Burns is credited with recruiting a number of Irish priests to serve in the diocese. It was also during Msgr. Burns' pastorate that St. Matthew's Church underwent renovations which included the addition of a gathering area, a baptistry and new entrance.

Father Luke McLoughlin is the current pastor of the parish which has grown to nearly 1,000 registered families.

# CHRIST THE KING

In 1954, the Diocese of Saint Augustine purchased land alongside the planned Arlington Expressway in Jacksonville. In February of 1955, the boundaries of Christ the King were officially erected as a parish by Archbishop Joseph P. Hurley.

As he looked out over the plots of land filled with scrub pine and palmetto bushes, the founding pastor, Father W. Thomas Larkin, could hardly foresee that his new parish would one day encompass 11 buildings, a thriving school, an outdoor shrine, and a community of diverse cultures bound by a deep devotion to one true faith.

Prior to building, the small community of 30 families had been worshipping in an auditorium at Jacksonville University. From the time when Msgr. John J. Lenihan, M.S.W. began his pastorate at Christ the King in 1968 to the time Msgr. Mortimer Danaher began his in 1978, the parish had grown to more than 200 families.

To meet these growing needs, a new church was dedicated on June 2, 1980 by Bishop John J. Snyder in the presence of Bishop Paul F. Tanner, Msgrs. Lenihan and Danaher and Most Rev. W. Thomas Larkin, Bishop of St. Petersburg and the founding pastor of Christ the King.

In 1992, Msgr. Danaher established the Sacrificial Giving Program, an initiative which encouraged parishioners to give ten percent of their income "back to the Lord." By participating in the program, parishioners enjoy the educational benefits of Christ the King School, Morning Star School, and Bishop Kenny High School.

In 1997, after 20 years of service at Christ the King, Msgr. Danaher retired as pastor. Father Robert J. Baker, S.T.D., was installed as Christ the King's new shepherd on Sept. 28, 1997. During the two short years he was pastor, he initiated a major construction project to improve and enlarge the elementary school. He also purchased a "House of Prayer" that include an "outdoor" Stations of the Cross for use by parishioners for prayer and meditation.

Currently, there are more than 45 ministries affiliated with Christ the King. During the 1980s and 1990s, a thriving Vietnamese Catholic community emerged in the diocese and began to call Christ the King their new home. The beloved Father Paul Van Tran was the first priestly leader of Vietnamese Catholics. Today, the entire parish, but especially the Vietnamese community, looks to Father Thanh Thai Nguyen for spiritual leadership. Father Thanh was named administrator of the parish in the fall of 1999, following Pope John Paul II's appointment of Father Robert Baker to Bishop of Charleston. The parish was delighted, yet sad to see their pastor of two years leave.

Father Robert J. McDermott was appointed on Sept. 27, 1999 by Bishop John J. Snyder as pastor of Christ the King which has grown to be one of the largest Catholic communities in Jacksonville with more than 2,400 registered families.

# ST. STEPHEN

## *Bunnell*

From 1914 to 1955, the Catholic residents of Bunnell, the county seat of Flagler County, had to travel to Korona for Sunday Mass. Beginning Sunday, May 15, 1955, that long cycle of treks was put to an end when the celebration of Mass moved to the Bunnell Civic Center.

Foreseeing Catholic growth in the area, in 1952 the diocese purchased a 14-acre tract of land on State Road 100. On Oct. 14, 1956, Msgr. John J. Fitzpatrick, the future bishop of Brownsville, and Father Vincent E. Smith, who shared the Bunnell post from St. Augustine, proposed to the Catholics of Bunnell that they build their own church on the selected property.

The cost for a church building was set at $30,000 and Msgr. Fitzpatrick announced that $10,000 had already been donated to the church by Frank J. Lewis of Chicago and Palm Beach, a wealthy benefactor of the Catholic Church Extension Society. Archbishop Joseph P. Hurley dedicated the church on May 13, 1957 and on that same day he confirmed an entire class of adults and children. "Love this church as your own spiritual home - not as a thing of brick and mortar, of wood and metal, not as a thing put together by human hands - but as a house of the Living God and the gateway through which your souls will pass into eternal life," said Hurley. A statue of the Blessed Virgin was donated by Eugene V. Smith of Philadelphia, father of St. Stephen's first permanent pastor, Father Vincent E. Smith.

The church was a monument to the Catholics of Bunnell, most of whom had limited financial resources and worked in the local cement factory, on lumber farms, in the turpentine industry, or farming potatoes. In fact, much of the heavy machinery employed in stripping the land for the building was provided by the men of the parish.

In 1965, Father Antonio Leon was appointed pastor to the 40-family parish. In 1974, Father Thomas Cody was appointed pastor followed by Fathers Roland Julien, Anthony Sebra, and Caesar Russo.

The current pastor is Father Frederick Parke of St. Elizabeth Ann Seton in Palm Coast.

# BLESSED TRINITY

*Jacksonville*

The first Mass in what is now Blessed Trinity Parish was celebrated by a small group of faithful Catholics on Nov. 9, 1958 in the Southside Estates Elementary School by Father James Gloekler, its founding pastor.

Encouragement to build a permanent church was enhanced when a local delegation of parents and ministers filed a legal request to expel the Catholics from gathering in the public school. The complaint was dismissed by the Duval County Court, but was later appealed by the Florida State Supreme Court. The State court dismissed the complaint based on the interim status of the elementary school scheme.

At last, Blessed Trinity was established as a parish on June 26, 1959 in response to the rapid growth of Jacksonville east of Assumption Parish.

By May of 1960 ground was broken for a new grade school. In 1967 a parish hall was built and in 1974 a new road to the church was constructed giving the property access from Beach Boulevard. Sadly, in 1971 the parish elementary school had to be closed due to a "lack of funding."

The 25th anniversary of the parish was celebrated in 1983 by Bishop John J. Snyder and Father Denis F. O'Regan, the present pastor. The homily was preached by Father John Gillespie, a son of the parish.

In May of 1992, a true milestone was reached when Bishop Snyder dedicated a new brick church. "As beautiful and imposing as this structure is," Bishop Snyder concluded, "it has meaning that transcends what our senses perceive for its planning, hard work, and sacrifices of so many ... How lovely is your dwelling place, O God!"

Father O'Regan, pastor since 1972, has seen the parish through shaky times to times of great prosperity. "May this building, consecrated today," Father O'Regan wrote in 1992, "be a living reality of our great faith." Truly, the faith of the parish is great and deep.

In 1999, the parish welcomed in a new elementary school in order to educate, "those who will follow when we have gone." Entering the Third Millennium, Blessed Trinity boasts nearly 800 registered Catholic families.

# RESURRECTION

*Jacksonville*

Resurrection Parish was founded between two milestones. In 1958, Catholic growth in Florida dictated a split of the Diocese of Saint Augustine and the formation of the Archdiocese of Miami.

In 1960, John Fitzgerald Kennedy, a Catholic who also acted as an usher at St. Edward Church in Palm Beach, was elected President of the United States. Clearly, Catholicism in America was coming of age and the area between Merrill Road and Fort Caroline was no exception to that growth.

Archbishop Joseph P. Hurley named Father James F. Gloekler in charge of founding a new parish community. The new parish was to serve the nearly 200 families living in the Jacksonville University area. For the first year of operation, the families met in the Swisher Auditorium of Jacksonville University.

In 1962, Father Gloekler was transferred and the young Father Matthew Connolly had a provisional church built near the university. The new church structure was completed in 1963, with all the families pledging money to cover cost of construction. Father Connolly celebrated the first parish Mass there on Feb. 17, 1963. In May of that same year, the church and school were dedicated. Inside, the church was decorated with a beautiful hand carved crucifix and six oak candlesticks imported from Rome.

Later in the 1960s, a social hall and two portable classrooms were added. And in May, 1979, a permanent church was dedicated.

In 1988, the parish added a one-million dollar gymnasium and parish center.

In 1996 a new rectory was dedicated that included offices for the parish priests. In the meantime, the church space in the first building was divided up to provide more classrooms and office space.

Resurrection was served well by many caring people including the Adrian Dominican Sisters. Also part of a great story of faith and love at Resurrection, the following priests served the parish community: James Gleockler (first pastor), Matthew Connolly, Joseph Barry, Eugene Kohls, Daniel Cody, Pat Sheedy, William Stahler, Vincent Haut, John Sullivan, Terrence Morgan, James Heslin, Jim Masterson, Mike Morse, Wayne Price, and Dan Shashy.

Father Tom Cody is the current pastor of Resurrection which has more than 1,000 families and 300 students enrolled in the school.

Resurrection has grown in many ways says Father Cody, adding, "We try to embrace the full vision of Vatican II. We empower our lay members to take ownership of their church and school and give richer expression to the presence of Jesus among us."

# SACRED HEART

## *Jacksonville*

Resurrection Parish was founded between two milestones. In 1958, Catholic growth in Florida dictated a split of the Diocese of Saint Augustine and the formation of the Archdiocese of Miami.

In 1960, John Fitzgerald Kennedy, a Catholic who also acted as an usher at St. Edward Church in Palm Beach, was elected President of the United States. Clearly, Catholicism in America was coming of age and the area between Merrill Road and Fort Caroline was no exception to that growth.

Archbishop Joseph P. Hurley named Father James F. Gloekler in charge of founding a new parish community. The new parish was to serve the nearly 200 families living in the Jacksonville University area. For the first year of operation, the families met in the Swisher Auditorium of Jacksonville University.

In 1962, Father Gloekler was transferred and the young Father Matthew Connolly had a provisional church built near the university. The new church structure was completed in 1963, with all the families pledging money to cover cost of construction. Father Connolly celebrated the first parish Mass there on Feb. 17, 1963. In May of that same year, the church and school were dedicated. Inside, the church was decorated with a beautiful hand carved crucifix and six oak candlesticks imported from Rome.

Later in the 1960s, a social hall and two portable classrooms were added. And in May, 1979, a permanent church was dedicated.

In 1988, the parish added a one-million dollar gymnasium and parish center.

In 1996 a new rectory was dedicated that included offices for the parish priests. In the meantime, the church space in the first building was divided up to provide more classrooms and office space.

Resurrection was served well by many caring people including the Adrian Dominican Sisters. Also part of a great story of faith and love at Resurrection, the following priests served the parish community: James Gleockler (first pastor), Matthew Connolly, Joseph Barry, Eugene Kohls, Daniel Cody, Pat Sheedy, William Stahler, Vincent Haut, John Sullivan, Terrence Morgan, James Heslin, Jim Masterson, Mike Morse, Wayne Price, and Dan Shashy.

Father Tom Cody is the current pastor of Resurrection which has more than 1,000 families and 300 students enrolled in the school.

Resurrection has grown in many ways says Father Cody, adding, "We try to embrace the full vision of Vatican II. We empower our lay members to take ownership of their church and school and give richer expression to the presence of Jesus among us."

# SAN JOSE

## *Jacksonville*

Plans for San Jose Parish began as early as 1954 when Archbishop Joseph P. Hurley anticipated that enormous growth would take place in an area located between Mandarin and downtown Jacksonville. He purchased 25 acres of land at the corner of Toledo and St. Augustine Roads and in February of 1959, Archbishop Hurley sent Father Mortimer Danaher to organize a parish.

At the time, personal contact was thought to be the only way to alert Catholics of the area that a new parish was being established. So he went door-to-door seeking new parishioners. An interim place of worship was established at the Bolles School and more than 300 people attended the Mass that was held in the school's gymnasium.

In September of 1959 Father Danaher organized a Women's Guild and the Sisters of St. Joseph began a Sunday CCD program for children.

In July of 1960, ground was broken for a temporary church facility. The first Mass was celebrated on Christmas Eve, 1960, and the church was dedicated by Archbishop Hurley in February of 1961.

Father Danaher turned to the Sisters of Mercy from Ireland to help establish a new school. In the summer of

1961, Mother M. Therese Horan and Sister Enda Egan and the late Sister De Montfort arrived to take the reins. Mother Horan served as the school's first principal.

In 1968, the noted St. Augustine artist Hugo Olms completed a shrine to the Holy Family that features an outdoor altar and fountains.

In 1977, Msgr. John J. Lenihan was appointed pastor. Under his leadership, the school was expanded to include more classrooms and a new library. And in October, 1990, through the dedication of Msgr. Lenihan and generations of parishioners, a new church was completed. It was dedicated by Bishop John J. Snyder in November of that year.

Built in the Spanish style of modern materials, the new church welcomes all to celebrate. Flanked by two chapels, the Blessed Sacrament Chapel and Our Lady of Guadalupe Chapel, the sanctuary received additional decoration with a handmade mosaic of Christ's Resurrection in 1988. "It is a home to hear the Word and to partake of the Sacrament," Msgr. Lenihan said about the new church building, adding that the parish was truly a "family of faith."

On June 15, 1999, Msgr. Lenihan retired as pastor and Father James Moss was appointed to succeed him in shepherding the 1,500 families who make San Jose their spiritual home.

# ST. PATRICK

*Jacksonville*

In 1958, Archbishop Joseph P. Hurley decided that North Jacksonville needed a parish to accommodate Catholic growth in the area. He purchased 39 acres to serve the area north of the Trout River, east of U.S. Route 1, and north to the Nassau County line. Originally, the large tract was to be the site of not only a parish, but also an elementary school, social hall, and eventually a Catholic high school.

To carry out his wishes, Hurley turned to a priest who had just arrived from the Dingle Peninsula in Ireland, Father John J. Lenihan. As founding pastor, he left a deep impression on the new parish community. With a smile on his face and a kind word on his tongue, he went door-to-door visiting the nearby neighborhood announcing that a new Catholic Church would soon be started.

Integral to the success of the parish was a core group of women who helped Father Lenihan canvass the neighborhoods for prospective parishioners. Until a permanent structure was built in 1960, Mass was celebrated on Sundays in the Ribault Lions Club auditorium and later at the Highlands Civic Center. The first and present church building saw its first Mass celebrated on July 10, 1960.

The next order of business was to build a school. After three years of successful fund-raising and sacrificial giving, a school was opened on Sept. 1, 1964. To staff the school, Father Lenihan looked homeward to secured the services of four Sisters of Mercy form County Tipperary. The sisters thrived in their new setting as they began educating and forming the faith of hundreds of parish children.

In 1967, the parish bade farewell to its "good and faithful servant," Father Lenihan. Father Michael Larkin was assigned to build upon Father Lenihan's success. But this was a time of considerable growth for the diocese and Father Larkin was soon called to found another parish, Prince of Peace, also in Jacksonville.

Father Larkin was succeeded by Fathers John Bender, Thomas Gordon, and John P. O'Flaherty. Father O'Flaherty built a new convent for the Mercy Sisters in 1978, balanced the parish books, and added the signature diocesan risen Christ behind the altar. In 1979 a new parish hall was dedicated in Father O'Flaherty's honor and a church renovation in 1984 marked a fitting tribute to Father O'Flaherty.

In 1990, Father Robert J. McDermott was assigned to St. Patrick's and was welcomed with the characteristic graciousness of the parish. While the contributions of parish priests are much more tangible than "brick and mortar," Father McDermott has of course built up the parish plant to meet the demands of a thriving parish community.

On May 1, 1997, a beautiful gymnasium and classroom building was dedicated by Bishop John J. Snyder. In October 1999, Bishop Snyder appointed Father Ronald Camarda pastor of St. Patrick's which has 400 registered families and a school enrollment of 270.

# ST. MARY, OUR MOTHER OF MERCY

Established 1960

## Macclenny

Prior to 1960, most Catholics in Baker County traveled to St. Edward Parish in Starke to attend to their weekly duties. As the Macclenny area continued to grow during the late 1950s, particularly following the construction of the Florida State Hospital, Archbishop Joseph P. Hurley began to explore ways to establish a parish in Macclenny.

On Dec. 8, 1958, on the Feast of the Immaculate Conception, a small cinder block chapel was dedicated. The St. Mary, Mother of Mercy Chapel, the first Catholic building in Baker County, signified the ministry of consolation which was attendant to its proximity to the State Hospital.

Father Joseph Maniangat, who was appointed pastor on Dec. 1, 1983, not only tended to the spiritual needs of the State Hospital, but to prisoners on death row at Florida State Prison in Raiford and state facilities. At the same time, with the help of other parishes in the diocese and grants, he and the parishioners built a beautiful new church. On Oct. 13, 1996, Bishop John J. Snyder officially blessed the church.

In 1999, Father Jose Maniyangat was appointed pastor of St. Mary, Mother of Mercy Parish which has about 175 registered families.

# MOST HOLY REDEEMER

Established 1962

## Jacksonville

The story of Most Holy Redeemer Parish is a story of cheerful growth. When Father Thaddeus McHugh was directed to establish a mission, or proto-parish, in the Normandy area of Jacksonville in 1962, he wrote to Archbishop Joseph P. Hurley for suggestions on naming the new mission. "Holy Redeemer," the archbishop scribbled on a memo pad, and that was it.

The first Mass in Most Holy Redeemer Parish was celebrated on April 8, 1962 at the Normandy Elementary School. Father McHugh was later granted permission to move into a small house on the property. "When it is cleaned up, it will be a suitable place to live," the missionary priest wrote.

By March of 1964, ground was broken for a new church and over the next two years, the parish community fashioned a beautiful and modern worship space. The entire parish helped with its construction. The new church was dedicated later that year with Father Frank Mouch celebrating the first Mass on Aug. 9,1964.

By 1973, a Religious Education building was constructed and the interior of the church was completely renovated in 1984. Long-standing pastors include: Fathers Daniel Cody, Luke McLoughlin, and currently Father Thomas Willis.

Today, Jacksonville's Catholic Filipino community has enriched the parish with a vibrant faith. Nearly 600 families are registered at the parish. And on May 23, 1999, Father Willis and the entire parish community broke ground for a new church, "so that this and future generations may know of our commitment in faith to the Triune God - the Father, Son, and Holy Spirit - and the holy Catholic Church."

# EPIPHANY

## *Lake City*

The first Catholic Mass in Lake City was celebrated in June of 1865 by Bishop Augustin Verot, then the Vicar Apostolic of Georgia and Florida. During the late 19th century the area was ministered by Father Joseph Hugon from Tallahassee .

By the 1920s a mission church was established and Mass was celebrated on a monthly basis. Essentially, the Catholics of Lake City represent one of the oldest faith communities in all of Florida. Up to 1944, the mission was administered from Immaculate Conception Church in Perry when Father Michael Kelly was assigned as Lake City's first resident priest.

In 1955, Father Patrick Malone arrived as the new pastor and by 1959 a new church and school were established. The Sisters of Mercy of Wexford, Ireland, staffed Epiphany School from 1960 to 1979, when the school was turned over to the Sisters of St. Joseph of St. Augustine and local lay administrators. School enrollment is about 150 students.

A new and larger church was completed in 1967, with the first Mass being celebrated on Christmas Eve, 1966, even though the structure was not yet finished. As the population of Lake City continued to grow, the parish and school expanded as

well. A rectory was built in 1975 by Father William Kelly.

The contemporary Catholic community of Lake City celebrated a "coming of age" with the dedication, in 1996, of the new Epiphany Catholic Church. Designed in a contemporary style, Bishop John J. Snyder dedicated the new church on Jan. 7, 1996 "with joy and heartfelt congratulations." Pastor Anthony Sebra, who worked tirelessly to see the project through, called the new structure "the center of and source for a life of faith and service."

In June, 1999, Father Michael Morse was named pastor of the 1,800-parishioner community.

# HOLY SPIRIT

*Jacksonville*

Jesus Is Laid In The Tomb

On Feb. 13, 1966, Father Richard J. Bowles offered the first Mass in the newly designated Holy Spirit Parish. The fledgling congregation had to gather at the Beacon Hills Club House until a suitable church facility was built.

By Summer of 1966, the congregation quickly outgrew the small clubhouse and the place of liturgy was changed to the Knights of Columbus Hall on Merrill Road. In November of 1968, Father Bowles was transferred and Father R. Joseph James was appointed the new pastor. Within three years a new church was erected. Bishop Paul F. Tanner dedicated the church on Oct. 3, 1971, hoping that the new house of God "would become an important part of every church members personal family life."

In 1974, a new rectory was built on Fort Caroline Road and in 1985 Bishop John J. Snyder appointed the present pastor, Msgr. James J. Heslin. "United in faith and love," Bishop Snyder wrote upon the occasion of Holy Spirit's 25th anniversary in 1991, "you meet here to be enlivened by His Word and to share in the body and blood of Our Savior. Truly, then, the Lord is present in this spot."

Over the years, Holy Spirit Parish has grown as a community of faith and love. On Sept. 20, 1992, Bishop John J. Snyder dedicated a new church to accommodate the more than 1,000 families registered at the parish. In addition, the Catholic school has an enrollment of about 300 students.

# ST. JOHN THE BAPTIST

## Established 1966

### *Atlantic Beach*

It was Feb. 25, 1966 when Archbishop Joseph P. Hurley affixed the diocesan seal to documents establishing St. John the Baptist Church in Atlantic Beach a parish community.

The Catholic presence at Mayport, however goes back more than a century before the church's founding. In 1860, a mission church was built in Mayport and attached to Immaculate Conception Church in downtown Jacksonville. During the Civil War, troops of the 8th Maine regiment headquartered in Jacksonville ransacked the small mission church, desecrated the vestments, and burned the church to the ground. After the Union Troops left, a new mission church was built and completed around 1870.

The new church was abandoned 25 years later along with a convent that was used by the Sisters of St. Joseph. The economy and the municipality were drying-up, and the church merely followed the constrictions of demography. By 1895, a new mission chapel was built a half mile from the coast to minister to the 100-parishioner community.

This new church served the community until 1940, when it, too, was destroyed to make way for the Mayport Naval Station. The Catholic community at Mayport gathered independently in homes and waited anxiously for the day when a new church would be built.

In 1955, a small chapel was donated and used until 1967, when a brick church was built on Mayport Road combining new space along with the hand-carved altar of the old 1955 chapel.

The parish celebrated its 25th anniversary in October 1992 with Bishop John J. Snyder noting that the celebration served as a "source of inspiration and pride to the People of God of Atlantic Beach."

St. John the Baptist pastoral leaders have included: Msgr. Joseph Dawson, Msgr. Vincent Haut, Msgr. Daniel Logan and Father Patrick Foley .

The current pastor, Father Joseph Meehan, presides over a thriving parish with about 700 registered families.

*The Last Supper as depicted in the frontal of the church altar.*

# ST. JOHN

## Interlachen

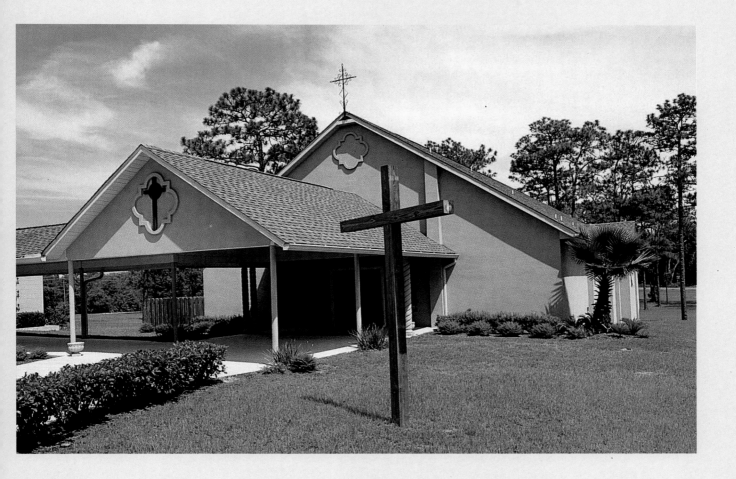

In 1958, the only place in Interlachen to celebrate Mass was the garage of a local Catholic family's home. For about 10 years, the Mass was celebrated on Saturday evenings. This schedule allowed the associate pastors from St. Monica Parish in Palatka to meet the sacramental obligations of the Interlachen flock as well as attend to the needs of the Palatka faithful.

Of course, over the years the strong-willed Catholics of Interlachen would sound a cry for a full-time priest. In 1963, a Sunday Mass was made available with St. John's becoming a mission church of St. Patrick Parish in Gainesville. In 1966, ground was broken for a church building and by 1970 St. John's had its first resident priest, Msgr. Thomas A. O'Reilly, a retired priest from Madison, Wisconsin.

Within a decade, the Catholics of Interlachen were clamoring for a true parish. The assignment of Father John "Jack" Heerey as resident pastor in 1983 gave more light to success. "We love Father Jack," the parishioners wrote to

Bishop John J. Snyder, "and we want him here full time!"

During the 1980s Father Jack presided over a "very alive spiritual community" which expanded "with open arms" to meet the demands of a new Hispanic Catholic population. Indeed, Father Jack's Christian sensitivity made the parish a model of social and spiritual good will.

In 1990, St. John's was granted parish status and a parish council was created. And on Feb. 5, 1995, a new church was dedicated by Bishop Snyder as a "permanent manifestation of the Catholic presence in the Interlachen area." Upon Father Heerey's second retirement, Father James O'Neal was assigned pastor in 1997.

Sadly, in 1999 "Father Jack" Heerey, beloved by all, died while visiting family in New York. As a magnificent tribute, some members of St. John's Parish traveled by car from Interlachen to New York to attend his funeral Mass.

Father James O'Neal is pastor of the parish which has about 200 families registered.

# SAN SEBASTIAN

## *St. Augustine*

"To build a church is a great thing ... a wonderful thing ... to pay it off is even better," Father John P. O'Flaherty wryly wrote in August of 1968 as the newly established parish of San Sebastian began construction.

During construction, Mass was celebrated in the Carcaba Flower Shop and later in a renovated barn donated by parishioner John Sugart. The small community however, continued to think large and bought the present parish acreage in 1969. By 1973, a brand new parish building, featuring the Spanish mission style, was dedicated by Bishop Paul F. Tanner with more than 600 participating in the blessing.

In 1980, a new day dawned on San Sebastian as the Order of Friars Minor Conventual, the Franciscans, were asked by Bishop John J. Snyder to take over the administration of the parish. In addition, the diocese was also looking to expand a ministry to the deaf community, and the Franciscans readily began a ministry to the deaf and blind. Franciscan Father Douglas Reed was named pastor in 1980.

While there was cause for many blessings for San Sebastian, decreasing numbers of vocations forced the Franciscans to relinquish the parish back to the diocese in 1993.

Father Peter Colasurdo was assigned as pastor shortly after. In 1996, a new interior renovation was completed. New tile was installed, and two large paintings by St. Augustine artist Joe Taylor were unveiled.

The parish continues to thrive, has a growing Hispanic ministry program, and looks to embrace future growth in the St. Augustine area. In October 1999, Bishop Snyder officially appointed Father Thomas Walsh pastor of San Sebastian, home to nearly 300 Catholic families.

# ST. MADELEINE

## *High Springs*

*The original church, located adjacent to the modern church seen below.*

followed by Father Michael Williams in 1971; Father Paul Hogarty in 1973; Father Roland Julien in 1974; Father John Dux in 1977; Father Joseph Meehan in 1985; Father Wayne Price in 1993; and Father Noel Cox, CSSp in May, 1995.

In 1979, the parish was moved to a new site just south of High Springs. The old church moved and a modern multi-purpose building was constructed, with its modern design standing in contrast to the white frame wooden church. The parish hall was dedicated on May 6, 1984.

In 1995, parishioner Marie Rizzi secured the abandoned Church of God by Faith building in Hawthorne and had it moved to High Springs. This building was renovated and made into a classroom for catechetical instruction.

As the parish moves toward the new millennium, it counts more than 300 families under the pastoral leadership of Father Noel Cox, CSSp.

O n April 9, 1969, Bishop Paul F. Tanner erected the parish of St. Madeleine Sophie in High Springs. Catholicism in High Springs, however, was nurtured much earlier than the date of its parish establishment. The first Mass in High Springs was held in the home of Sarah and James Paul. Although Paul was a Presbyterian, he and his wife had great respect and regard for each others beliefs. They moved from Savannah, Georgia in 1906.

The parish was named for St. Madeleine Sophie Barat, a French woman who in 1800 founded the Society of the Sacred Heart. In April 1925, the same year Madeleine Sophie was canonized a saint by Pope Pius XI, James Paul, deeded land to the Diocese of Saint Augustine so the first Catholic Church in High Springs could be built.

Draper Underwood was given the contract to build the church and it was dedicated six weeks later. The pews and kneelers in the church were also constructed by Hunt, who crafted them after the folding chairs in the church began "folding at the wrong time."

As a mission church, the chapel was served by priests from St. Patrick Parish in Gainesville. In 1968, Father Richard Altenbaugh became the first resident pastor in High Springs. He was

# ST. CATHERINE

*Orange Park*

The Catholic presence in Orange Park has revolved around St. Catherine Parish since the time of Bishop John Moore. In 1877, a plot of land was purchased on the corner of Reed and Stowe avenues and a small wooden church was constructed. This white wooden church was consecrated in 1877 under the name of St. Catherine and administered from its mother church, Immaculate Conception in Jacksonville.

The mission has gone through cycles based on the number of Catholics in the area. It was almost dismantled in 1900, but with the founding of Moosehaven in 1903, visitations were resumed on a bi-weekly basis. In 1930, a renovation of the wooden mission chapel was undertaken with the installation of gas lighting, a wood stove, and a portable organ.

"Orange Park is not growing very fast, I must say," Father Joseph Corde wrote in 1963. But he spoke a little too soon. Within the next 10 years the opening of the Buckman Bridge would transform Orange Park into a veritable boom town.

On Feb. 24, 1970, Bishop Paul F. Tanner elevated St. Catherine's to parish status and assigned Father Edward Rooney its first pastor. His successor, Msgr. R. Joseph James, presided over the construction of a new modern, fan-shaped church. And on June 7, 1981, Bishop John J. Snyder dedicated the new church of St. Catherine on Kingsley Avenue.

In 1983, Msgr. Vincent Haut was assigned pastor and continues to shepherd one of the fastest growing parishes in the diocese. In 1987, a new Christian Formation Center was constructed. The parishioners of St. Catherine are committed to meeting the needs of both their parish and Orange Park community. Among the many ministries at the parish, there is a thriving youth ministry, Hispanic ministry, and an annual Urban Plunge program, a youth-run ministry for the inner city poor. Parishioners also provide many other outreach services to the poor and hungry. The 3,000 registered families hope to be worshiping in an expanded St.Catherine's Church soon in the Third Millennium.

# PRINCE OF PEACE

**Established 1970**                                    *Jacksonville*

served by Father Michael Larkin, pastor, since its founding on June 10, 1970," the ceremonial invitation read. After 25 years, Father Larkin noticed that "the parish has had the powerful witness of founders, former parishioners, and its present family members who know `How good it is for us to be here." (Mk 9:5).

About 1,450 parishioners are registered at Prince of Peace.

*Below, a full emersion baptismal font, the first to be built in the diocese.*

When Bishop Paul F. Tanner established the boundaries of Prince of Peace Parish in June of 1970, America's war in Vietnam was raging across the seas while peacefulness settled over the scrub brush and pines that would become Jacksonville's newest parish community.

Father Michael J. Larkin and members of the new parish broke ground on a rainy morning in November of 1972. There was one thought on their minds, "From Woods to Worship. " They had committed themselves to having the new church built within one year. Indeed, On Dec. 5, 1973 the new church was dedicated by Bishop Tanner.

Through the years, the parish has made vigilant efforts to preserve peace. During the July 4th weekend of 1980, the parish held a prayer vigil service for the American hostages who were being held captive in Iran. On that occasion, Bishop John J. Snyder wrote to the parish asking them to "pray that our country recommit itself to be an instrument of peace in our troubled world."

On June 11, 1995, the now robust parish celebrated a joyous 25th anniversary. "Our parish is proud to have been

# SANTA MARIA DEL MAR

## *Flagler Beach*

**Established 1970**

Even though the small town of Flagler Beach registered only 600 voters in 1954, the prospective growth in the area spurred Catholic development with the Diocese of Saint Augustine purchasing land.

By 1966, the first Mass was celebrated in Flagler Beach by Father Antonio Leon in a renovated building known as the "Blessed Sacrament Chapel." Within months, Father Leon drew up plans for a new structure and ground was broken in 1970.

On Oct. 11, 1970, the first Mass was celebrated in the new church and Bishop Paul F. Tanner dedicated the building on Dec. 3, 1970. Soon after, Father Leon noticed a great deal of growth was taking place in the Palm Coast area and he urged the diocese to begin investing in the area by purchasing land which eventually became St. Elizabeth Ann Seton Parish.

Father Thomas Cody was assigned as pastor in 1974 and served there for three years. Father Cody holds the distinction of having celebrated the first baptism at Santa Maria del Mar Parish. Father Roland Julien succeeded Father Cody in 1977 and served as pastor until 1980.

Father Anthony Sebra arrived in 1980 and was responsible for introducing the "Renew" program to parishioners. He also installed stained-glass windows, created a recreation area, and renovated the interior of the church.

In 1990, Father John P. O'Flaherty was assigned as pastor. "Never before have I experienced so many parishioners so willing to help their parish and their pastor," said Father O'Flaherty on the occasion of the parish's 25th anniversary in 1995.

Today, the parish now serves more than 1300 parishioners in winter months and more than 700 during the summer. Completion of a new church is expected to take place early in the new millennium.

# OUR LADY STAR OF THE SEA

Established 1972

## *Ponte Vedra Beach*

On Oct.10, 1972, Bishop Paul F. Tanner officially erected Our Lady Star of the Sea Parish in Ponte Vedra Beach. Shortly after, Msgr. T. Leo Danaher arrived in Ponte Vedra Beach to put some real estate behind the parish that had been established on paper.

Immediately, he purchased 12 acres along Route A1A. Seventy-three Catholic families served as the core of the parish. Just two years later, the church was built and the first Mass celebrated on Christmas Eve 1974. Contractor Carroll Browning and other men of the parish helped build the rectory in 1976.

In 1979, a parish recreation center was constructed and named after Mr. Browning. In a major tribute to the generosity of the parish, on Jan. 26, 1984, the 10-year-old debt of the parish was retired. Bishop John J. Snyder presided at the Mass, while afterward Msgr. Danaher took delight in torching the mortgage. Much of the growth of the parish facilities was supplemented by voluntary labor, materials, and gifts provided by the parishioners.

Yet in the midst of prosperity, the parish's outreach to the poor was not sidetracked. In 1978, the parish sponsored two homeless people who were eking out an existence in nearby Palm Valley. The parish built them an entire new home, complete with central heat and air conditioning, appliances, and furnishings.

An Education Building was built in the 1980s. In the early 1990s, the church and the rectory were remodeled and in 1996, a beautiful Cultural Center was built.

In 1999, Msgr. Danaher and Bishop Snyder commemorated another high point for the parish with the dedication of the Palmer Catholic Academy of Our Lady Star of the Sea. On the occasion of the dedication of the new school, Bishop Snyder pointed out that the new parish school represented the efforts of the entire parish community and was an "opportunity for all parishioners of Our Lady Star of the Sea to share in something of lasting value: the education and religious formation of children."

Also in that year the parish's founder, Msgr. Danaher retired with the loving good wishes of his parish community. From 1972 to 1999 the parish had grown from 73 families to more than 1,850 families. Monsignor Daniel B. Logan serves as the second pastor of Our Lady Star of the Sea.

# HOLY FAITH

## Gainesville

On March 1, 1973, Bishop Paul F. Tanner established Holy Faith Parish in Gainesville and assigned Father Flannan Walsh pastor. From 1973 to 1976, Mass was celebrated at the Gainesville Women's Club facilities while Father Walsh finally settled on property for a parish plant in 1975.

The Holy Faith Social Hall and Education Building were dedicated by Bishop Tanner in November of 1976 and were quickly converted for celebration of the Eucharist. The parish came of age in February of 1982 when a new church was dedicated by Bishop John J. Snyder. According to Bishop Snyder, the People of God of the parish showed a witness of faith, vitality, and vibrancy. Seating close to 800 people, the new Holy Faith was shaped in the style of a pagoda, with the ceiling rising to a Maltese Cross. Tapestries in the church were donated by Barbara Ebersole of Gainesville.

In 1987, Msgr. R. Joseph James succeeded Father Walsh as pastor. Father Michael Williams was named pastor in 1990.

With the help of then-associate pastors Fathers Thomas Willis and Moises Palaroan, Fr. Williams established new programs for the youth of the parish and its diverse population, including Filipino and Hispanic parishioners.

In 1995, Father Williams and the parish helped to sponsor one of the city's Habitat for Humanity projects. Under Father William's leadership, the parish has stayed true to its mission statement, "to be a caring Christian community consistently giving thanks to God."

Nearly 1,550 families are registered at Holy Faith Parish.

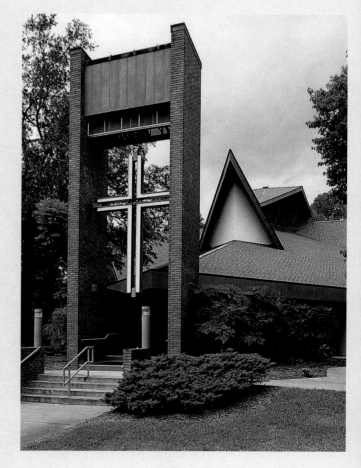

# ST. WILLIAM

## Keystone Heights

In 1949, Father Roman Rastatter of St. Edward Parish in Starke began traveling to Keystone Heights to celebrate Mass at the behest of a few Catholic families. By 1950, the Keystone Inn was rented for Sunday Mass and attendance increased. When the number grew to12 families, the Keystone Heights Women's Club building was rented and serious efforts were launched to purchase land to establish a parish.

Two entire city blocks were purchased in 1955 and Archbishop Joseph P. Hurley dedicated the new mission chapel on Feb. 16, 1955. At the time of the dedication, the walls were not yet painted and the front doors had not even been put in place; but at the end of the nave a special niche was created for the Blessed Sacrament.

On Sept. 3, 1973, Bishop Paul F. Tanner raised St. William from a mission to a parish and appointed Father Michael

Williams its first pastor.

With 124 families, a parish council was established, a census was taken, and a plan for a permanent church was initiated. On June 10, 1979, a new fan-shaped Church of St. William was dedicated in Keystone Heights by Bishop Tanner. In 1981, the parish entered into a progressive "Parish Covenant" with St. Anne Episcopal Church in Keystone Heights. The covenant was a call for the two parishes to work together in the community and to further the connective aspects of Catholicism and Episcopalianism. Father Williams left St. William's in 1985, and was succeeded by Father Tom Gordon, now deceased. Father Moises B. Palaroan is the present pastor and presides over a growing, vibrant, and spiritually vital parish with about 350 families.

# CHURCH OF THE CRUCIFIXION

**Established 1974**

## *Jacksonville*

Crucifixion Parish was established by Bishop Paul F. Tanner on Dec.12, 1974, but its history goes back 15 years prior to its canonical formation. As early as 1959, the pioneer families of the parish established what was known as the "North Jacksonville Mission," as an outreach of St. Pius V Parish. Soon, the little mission was showing signs of growth and deep spirituality. In 1963 there were 175 people registered and a catechism class.

"Many times, people are left standing during the Mass," members of the mission wrote to Archbishop Joseph P. Hurley as they petitioned for a permanent pastor. In 1970, a new mission church was opened on Edgewood Avenue in Jacksonville. Four years later, Bishop Tanner raised the mission to a permanent parish. Its care was entrusted to the Josephite Fathers who were administering St. Pius V Parish.

Father William Hogan was appointed first pastor. Father Matthew J. O'Rourke, SSJ, the Superior General of the Josephites, was personally convinced that Crucifixion Parish had "great potential."

In 1988, Father Cletus M. S. Watson, T.O.R. Franciscan, was welcomed as pastor and is presently serving as the beloved pastor of the parish. By 1990, the parish was sponsoring adult education classes, an active youth group, a parish council, and the Knights and Ladies of St. Peter Claver. In 1994, Crucifixion celebrated its 20th anniversary as a parish with Bishop John J. Snyder presiding as main celebrant and homilist for the historic occasion.

On Dec. 12, 1999, the 125 families registered at the Church of the Crucifixion celebrated their 25th anniversary.

# OUR LADY OF CONSOLATION

Established 1974

*Callahan*

In the 1930s, the "Ripley's Believe it or Not" novelty newspaper column reported that the smallest Catholic church in the United States was located in Callahan, Florida. The Catholic graveyard chapel at Callahan seated just six people.

In 1953, a group of Catholic families in Callahan decided to invite priests into their homes for the celebration of Mass. The Parisian family hosted the first communal Mass in Callahan which was celebrated by Father Joseph F. Ketter. As the congregation grew, Mass was said in the old Brandies Building, the Page Building, and even at the C&C grocery store.

Finally, in 1957, a new church was built and dedicated as Our Lady of Consolation, a mission church of St. Michael Parish in Fernandina. The communal spirit of the parish was exhibited early on, as parishioners donated and fashioned candles, tapestries, altar linens and sacred vessels. It remained a mission until October 1974, when Father Jerome Hickey was appointed pastor. The first confirmation was on Nov. 23, 1975 by Bishop Paul F. Tanner. In 1976, a beautiful grotto was built by parishioner Tom Sares and

dedicated on the occasion of Father Hickey's 35th anniversary of ordination to the priesthood. The grotto was subsequently moved to the new parish site.

In 1985, Bishop John J. Snyder appointed Father Ralph Besendorfer, J.C.D., the judicial vicar of the diocese as administrator of Our Lady of Consolation. Father Besendorfer had a vision to expand the parish and by 1992, a 14-acre parcel was purchased for the construction of a new church. On April 19, 1998, the new Our Lady of Consolation Church was dedicated by Bishop Snyder. Some of the stained-glass windows were crafted in Germany at the turn of the century and were originally in the first Holy Rosary Church building in Jacksonville. Others were donated by San Jose Parish in Jacksonville. While the new church is certainly magnificent and beautiful, Father Besendorfer reminded the parishioners that the true "beauty of our church community is found in its relationships." Bishop Snyder noted that the new church will stand as "a permanent manifestation of the Catholic presence in Callahan."

Our Lady of Consolation has 175 registered families.

# HOLY FAMILY

*Williston*

In 1962, Father Paul Couming wrote to Archbishop Joseph P. Hurley requesting that the Diocese of Saint Augustine seriously consider establishing a mission to minister to Catholics in Williston.

At that time, there were only 10 Catholic families in Williston and it took a ride to Ocala in order for them to meet their Sunday obligation. Twelve acres of land for a parish site was purchased in 1970. Within the year, the so-called "Tri-County Parish," consisting of the missions of High Springs, Cross City, and Williston were about to come of age.

For Williston, it was decided in May of 1971 that a future church would take the name of Holy Family. By 1975, the first permanent church building was dedicated and Father John Gillespie was appointed the first pastor of Holy

Family Church. Father Anthony Sebra served as pastor in 1979 and was followed by Father Patrick Foley.

Monsignor R. Joseph James presided over the 10th anniversary of the parish in 1985 when it boasted more than 225 families. Monsignor James was instrumental in establishing Cursillo, a retreat movement, and a sound stewardship program while in Williston.

Father Nicholas Glisson served as pastor from 1987 to 1991. Fathers John Pollard and James Moss helped to move the parish into the next decade by increasing outreach programs to youth and enhancing the Christian Formation Program.

In September, 1999, Bishop John J. Snyder appointed Father Paul Donnelly the new pastor of Holy Family Parish. It has more than 700 registered members

# CORPUS CHRISTI

Established 1975

## St. Augustine

Prior to its establishment as a parish, Corpus Christi was a mission station of St. Ambrose parish in Elkton. In June of 1976, the small mission was honored to welcome Bishop Paul F. Tanner to celebrate the Mass of the Feast of Corpus Christi at the mission church. Bishop Tanner was impressed with the rapid growth of the area and the deep spirituality of its Catholics. Consequently, Bishop Tanner established Corpus Christi as a parish on Nov. 14, 1977.

Father William C. Mooney was appointed administrator of the parish in 1977. That same year, Father Mooney rented a garage on Phoenetia Drive in St. Augustine Shores so that daily Mass could be celebrated. The rent was paid by a group of parishioners each month. "It was very cold in the winter, and very hot in the summer," said Father Mooney. Adding "In all its simplicity, with the rafters clearly visible, it reminded one of the stable at Bethlehem."

The next location for Mass was a cardroom followed by the poolroom at the Riverview Club in St. Augustine Shores. Eventually Mass was said in the main hall of the Riverview Club. "In circumstances, such as these, one had to be very flexible," said Father Mooney. On one occasion, he noted that "the props for Murder in the Cathedral, the story of St. Thomas Becket, were set up in the main hall. I put the perplexed manager of the club at ease by assuring him we would adjust to the circumstances. As I said Mass against the backdrop of the props for Murder in the Cathedral, I prayed that history would not be repeated!," said Father Mooney.

Father Mooney, known widely for his pastoral sensibilities, began a parish council under the leadership of Richard Waler as president. He also started classes in catechesis and programs for youth. Additionally, the parish has reached out to the retired members of the parish, many of whom have relocated to St. Augustine Shores from the heavily populated Catholic areas of the Northeast.

In 1980, Father Mooney was appointed pastor. As a mark of the community's zeal and Christian cooperation, a permanent church was dedicated by Bishop John J. Snyder on April 30, 1981. The fan-shaped church has a peaked ceiling at the end of the nave and is decorated by Italian linden wood statuary.

Prior to building a new administration building on church grounds, two borrowed homes and two rented houses were used. Father Mooney, with a little tongue-in-cheek wit, would say to his parishioners, "I know we are a pilgrim church, but are we not overdoing it?"

A parish hall was completed in 1999. The parish has about 700 registered families.

# HOLY FAMILY

In June of 1974, Bishop Paul F. Tanner sent Msgr. Daniel B. Logan a check for $3,000 and encouraged him to establish the "new Baymeadows Mission Church." Within six months, Msgr. Logan had decided to purchase a parcel of land along Baymeadows Road and began celebrating Mass in the Jacksonville Country Day School. The next order of business was to settle upon a name for the new parish. An early proposal was "St. Mary of the Woods," which Bishop Tanner discouraged as "ambiguous" and, given the fact that suburban sprawl has all but depleted the wooded areas of Baymeadows, the name of Holy Family wisely became the favorite.

In 1977 a building-fund drive was initiated by Msgr. Logan to build "a home for God — a proper edifice in which to honor him and grow in love and service to the Lord." As a tribute to the speed with which both pastor and parish responded to the spiritual needs of the community, the new Holy Family Catholic Church was dedicated on May 6, 1979. The new structure with a peaked wooden roof and modern stained glass was blessed by Bishop Tanner with Msgr. Logan concelebrating at the Mass of dedication.

Since its dedication, the Church of the Holy Family has continued to grow in spirit and numbers. In 1983, a new rectory was built and in 1986, a spacious parish center was dedicated. The parish council has taken an active role in parish life. Outreach to the poor, youth, Catholic singles, and divorced Catholics have been instituted. In 1988, the entire parish community joined in the celebration of the Silver Jubilee of Priestly Ordination of Msgr. Logan. Later, in the 1990s, an addition to the church was constructed to provide more seating and to provide other amenities such as a gathering area.

In 1999, parishioners gathered to celebrate the parish's 25th anniversary. And, at the same time to say farewell to their beloved founding pastor, Msgr. Logan, who was appointed pastor of Our Lady Star of the Sea Parish in Ponte Vedra Beach. Msgr. Logan left a thriving and active parish for Father Gregory Fay, who was graciously welcomed in June 1999 by the Holy Family community. Holy Family has about 876 registered families.

# ST. ELIZABETH ANN SETON

## *Palm Coast*

**Established 1979**

Early in 1974, Father Thomas Cody was asked by Bishop Paul F. Tanner to start a mission station in Palm Coast. From 1974 to 1976, Father Cody was a busy man, dividing his pastoral duties between St. Stephen Church in Bunnell and the new mission in Palm Coast. During these years, Mass was celebrated at the Palm Coast Welcome Center, the Palm Coast Fire Station, the YMCA, and even the local Lutheran church. At last, on May 13, 1979, a church structure was dedicated and named for St. Elizabeth Ann Seton, the first American-born saint. Parishioners then, as now, commonly refer to their church as "Mother Seton."

Palm Coast and its environs were host to a rapid rise in Catholic population spurred by the ITT Corporation's development of Palm Coast as a resort community. Within the span of 10 years, the Catholics of Palm Coast skyrocketed from about 70 people to more than 700 families in 1985, when Father Caesar Russo took over the reins from Father Cody as pastor.

By 1986, the parish boasted an active Women's Guild, a strong Cursillo movement, an outreach to the poor, a Men's Club, and a Knights of Columbus chapter. During the late 1980s Father Russo laid a sound financial foundation for future parish growth.

In 1992 Father Frederick R. Parke was assigned pastor of Mother Seton and moved the parish toward the dedication of a grand new church. When Bishop John J. Snyder dedicated the new church in January of 1994, the edifice ranked as the largest Catholic church in the diocese and in all of North Florida.

Palm Coast is the nation's largest planned community. Its population of 32,000 includes a diverse demographic mix. In 1999, Mother Seton opened a new school building, with 16 classrooms, and the parish expects, early in the new millennium, to steadily fill its pre-K through eighth grades. As the parish enters the Third Millennium, there are more than 3,500 families at St. Elizabeth Ann Seton.

# ST. FRANCIS XAVIER

## Established 1979

### Live Oak

Catholicism in Live Oak traces its history back to the early Spanish explorers who traveled the Apalachee Indian trials in northwest Florida. With the demise of the Franciscan missions, however, Catholic influence ebbed and it was not until the early 20th century that a new presence was established.

In 1910, Bishop William J. Kenny purchased two lots for future development and in 1914 Bishop Michael Curley purchased an additional lot. In 1915, an old wooden school building was moved to the new church property and refurbished as a church. In 1916, the new mission was named "Saints Margaret and Elizabeth" and was attended by priests from Tallahassee.

Some four decades later, in 1952, the little mission's name was inexplicably changed to St. Francis Xavier. During the 1940s and into the 1950s the mission was attended to by priests from Immaculate Conception Church in the town of Perry.

By 1962, the old one-room church was deteriorating beyond repair. It was so bad, that Mass was held on the front

lawn of the church! To celebrate Mass in a protected space, the Live Oak Elks Lodge was used by Father Patrick Malone of Epiphany Parish in Lake City. Following the sale of the old parish property, a new church building was built in 1963 at the present location. The new church was administered by Father William A. Kelly from Epiphany Parish.

In 1979, Bishop Paul F. Tanner established St. Francis Xavier as its own parish and assigned Father N. Edward Booth as its first resident pastor. Father Booth established a lay parish council, started a youth ministry program, and built a rectory. In 1984, Father James O'Neal was named pastor of St. Francis. Father O'Neal started a parish library, adult education courses and began a Spanish Mass for the Hispanic community of Suwannee and Lafayette counties.

In 1991, Father Michael Morse was appointed pastor and continued to expand the Hispanic ministry. He also enlarged both the church and the rectory. About 400 families are members of the St. Francis Xavier Parish community.

In 1999 Father Morse was named pastor of Epiphany Parish in Lake City and Father Michael Pendergraft was appointed pastor of St. Francis Xavier Parish.

# ST. LUKE

*Middleburg*

On Aug. 24, 1982, Bishop John J. Snyder established St. Luke Parish in Middleburg. However, the Catholic presence here dates to 1859, when Bishop Augustin Verot proudly wrote to his superiors at the Society for the Propagation of the Faith in Rome, that "Middleburg has a church."

By the turn of the century, the little church at Middleburg was served by priests from the Cathedral in St. Augustine and Immaculate Conception Church in Jacksonville.

Over time, the small congregation dwindled, but by 1972, the Catholic population in Middleburg was on the rise. They made known their interest in establishing a mission to Father Edward Rooney, then pastor of St. Catherine Parish in Orange Park. At that time, more than 40 families registered at St. Catherine's were from the Middleburg area.

In 1973, Father Luke McLoughlin was assigned to the mission and he began celebrating Mass in the Middleburg Civic Center. In 1976, Father McLoughlin purchased the old Baptist church in Orange Park and moved the building to Middleburg. After a renovation, the new church was ready for services for the growing community.

In 1982, Father Edward Rooney was appointed pastor of St. Luke Parish. In 1986, a parish center was built to serve as both a worship space and for other pastoral purposes. Currently, the parish has grown to more than 900 families and plans are on the drawing board to build a new church.

St. Luke Parish grounds are also home to the Annunciation Interparish School, with grades pre-K through eight, which serves the parishes of St. Luke, St. Catherine in Orange Park and Sacred Heart in Green Cove Springs.

# SAN JUAN DEL RIO

## Switzerland

In December of 1976, Msgr. Joseph Dawson suggested to the diocese that a mission church be started adjacent to Camp St. John, where Catholic summer youth camps had been operated by the diocese since 1959.

The camp, originally known as the Hodges Estate, was part of a 110-acre land purchase made by Archbishop Joseph P. Hurley in 1958. On the estate was also a manor house, made of coquina stone. It was called the Hodges Mansion and it overlooks the St. Johns River.

Near the camp were the growing Switzerland and Fruit Cove communities of Jacksonville as noted by Msgr. Dawson. Now retired, Msgr. Dawson celebrated Mass in the game room of the mansion which would seat about 120. The first Mass was celebrated at the Hodges Mansion on Feb. 6, 1977.

In 1979, Father Gregory Fay was named administrator and began a renovation of the Hodges Mansion to meet the needs of a growing Catholic population. Meanwhile, there would be time to raise money to build a new church. In 1983, the mission was raised to a parish and attendance continued to increase. Parishioners at this time set out to build an all-purpose facility to function as both a church and parish hall. The Spanish-style building is used for worship, education, and social affairs. The Mass of dedication was celebrated on Sept. 11, 1988.

As housing in the area continued to develop, more families were joining the parish and in 1995 an elementary school was opened. Three years later, the school was expanded to include grades pre-K through eight. San Juan del Rio serves more than 1,000 families.

The continued growth has led the parish to develop plans for a larger church building. When it is constructed, it will make use of furnishings in the existing church.

In June of 1999, the parish bid a fond farewell to its founding pastor, Father Gregory Fay, who was named pastor of Holy Family Parish in Jacksonville. Today, Father N. Edward Booth is pastor of the parish.

# ST. ANASTASIA

## St. Augustine

I n May of 1985, Bishop John J. Snyder directed Msgr. Joseph Dawson to establish a new mission due to "growth and development in the Crescent Beach area."

The pioneer spirit of Catholics in the southern area of St. Augustine shone brightly as they gathered for the mission's first Mass on Oct. 6, 1985 in the Anastasia-Sheraton Inn. There were less than 100 registered Catholic parishioners, but growth continued due to the large number of visitors that attended Mass each weekend.

Three years later on Oct. 9, 1988, Bishop John J. Snyder dedicated a new mission church on Neff Road near Route A1A in St. Augustine. In 1991, Msgr. Dawson retired and Father Seamus O'Flynn was appointed pastor. Father O'Flynn was no stranger to St. Augustine for he had served as president of St. Joseph Academy since 1983.

Building on the solid spiritual and financial foundations laid down by Msgr. Dawson, Father O'Flynn began to develop plans for an even larger church to accommodate the

rapid upward demographic shift in St. Augustine. By 1992 the number of registered families had grown to 300 and with the assistance of architect, Walter O'Kon, a plan to extend the church to the capacity of 550 seats was developed. The new extension included: St. Anthony Hall, a fully equipped kitchen, a suite of offices for the pastor and ancillary services. The cost of the building was approximately $350,000 and it was completed in January of 1993, ready to accommodate the "snowbirds" that year.

By 1996, there were more than 2,000 Catholics attending

the temporary church structure built 10 years earlier. A grand new church was designed by Architect, Richard San Giovanni to reflect the Spanish heritage of St. Augustine with its coquina exterior, Spanish tile roofs and decorative stone facings. The new St. Anastasia Church, seating 1,569 people, was dedicated by Bishop John J. Snyder on Sept. 29, 1999. At a cost of about $4.5 million, St. Anastasia is one of the larger churches in the diocese.

A time capsule is located in the altar platform and is to be opened in the year 2049. It contains memorabilia collected since 1985 by both parishioners and the local community. More than 2,600 parishioners are registered at St. Anastasia Parish, where a large contingent of "snowbirds" still call the parish their home away from home.

# ST. JOHN THE EVANGELIST

### Established 1987

## *Chiefland*

Father Paul B. Hogarty celebrated the first Mass in Chiefland in December of 1973 at the Chief Theatre on Park Avenue. In 1974, Father Roland Julien of St. Madeleine's Tri-County Parish succeeded Father Hogarty and moved the Mass celebration to the Chiefland Recreational Center.

In 1975, Chiefland became a mission of St. Madeleine Parish in High Springs. In 1977, Father John Dux was assigned to Chiefland and the congregation continued to grow. In the spirit of ecumenism, Father Dux approached the First United Methodist Church of Chiefland and entered into an agreement for Mass to be celebrated there. From 1977 to 1982, Fathers Anthony Sebra and John Gillespie also served as pastors.

Bishop John J. Snyder officially dedicated a new mission church at Chiefland in September of 1982. Five years later, there were more than 100 families registered at the mission. St. John the Evangelist was raised to a formal parish in 1987. In 1989, Father Michael Pendergraft was appointed administrator. The following year, Father Pendergraft persevered through the process of building a new rectory and in 1993, Father Pendergraft was named pastor.

Currently, the parish ministers to more than 200 families. The parish council is planning a new library and classrooms for religious education. In June of 1999, the parish welcomed its new pastor, Father Joseph Maniangat.

# MARY, QUEEN OF HEAVEN

### Established 1988

## *Jacksonville*

In the Marian year of 1988 and after consultation with the Catholics of the former "Catholic Mission in Argyle Forest," Bishop John J. Snyder gave the name "Queen of Heaven" to the new church. When the mission was raised to a parish, Father Frank Haryasz, a retired U.S. Navy chaplain, was appointed its first pastor.

With 39 Catholics in attendance, the first Mass was celebrated on Sept. 18, 1988 at the Best Western Motel in Orange Park. A parish council was established in 1989, along with committees for liturgy and hospitality. More than 13 acres of land on Staples Mill Road was purchased in 1990 and in 1993 ground was broken for the Mary, Queen of Heaven Religious and Social Center.

In 1996, Queen of Heaven's founding pastor, Father Haryasz, was named pastor emeritus and Msgr. R. Joseph James was appointed pastor. Monsignor James has continued to lead the parish, which numbers some about 400 registered families, in deep spirituality and plans for future growth.

# QUEEN OF PEACE

## *Gainesville*

On March 23, 1988, Bishop John J. Snyder formally erected a new parish in Gainesville. Since 1988 was a Marian year for the universal Church, the new parishioners welcomed the name Queen of Peace. Nearly 100 families banded together to form the new parish under their first pastor, Father Flannan Walsh.

Since 1987, the community had been meeting for Mass at the Oak Hall School and, in the spirit of ecumenism, at the Fort Clark Baptist Church. In 1989, Father John Patrick, a retired United States Air Force Chaplain, joined the parish and endeared himself to all. Father Thomas Moore served as interim administrator of the parish.

In 1992, a beautiful new worship space and multi-purpose parish center was dedicated and Mass in Spanish was provided.

In 1994, Father Jeff McGowan was appointed as administrator and immediately started working with parishioners to begin laying the groundwork for the future. A comprehensive parish survey was conducted to determine the interest and needs of the ever-growing community. Results of the survey laid a foundation for deciding the future direction and projects of the parish. As the parish continued to reach out to young families, the parish grew and so did enthusiasm and visions.

In 1996, Queen of Peace parishioners began working on their next big project — to build a permanent church and add a second interparish school to the Gainesville area. This second school will pave the way for the first Catholic

Gainesville high school. The school will open in the fall of 2000. The permanent church building will open its doors to worship in early 2001.

Father McGowan was appointed pastor in June, 1999. Father J. Edgar Bayona joined the parish team as parochial vicar in September, 1999. More than 1,200 families are registered at Queen of Peace Catholic Community.

# MISSION NOMBRE DE DIOS

## St. Augustine

**Established 1565**

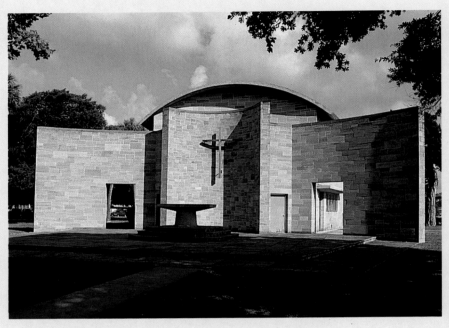

The Mission of Nombre de De dios traces its origins to the founding of the City of St. Augustine, America's oldest City, in 1565. On Sept. 8, 1565, Pedro Menéndez de Aviles landed and proclaimed this site for Spain and the Catholic Church. It was here that Menéndez knelt to kiss a wooden cross presented to him by Father Francisco Lopez de Mendoza Grajales, chaplain of his expedition. It was on these grounds that Father Lopez would celebrate the first parish Mass and begin the work at America's first Mission. It was at this sacred spot that the Spanish settlers would begin the devotion to Our Lady of la Leche that continues into the present.

*Most visitors to Mission Nombre de De dios begin their tour or pilgrimage at the Prince of Peace Church, located at the San Marco Avenue entrance to the grounds. The church was built in 1965 to commemorate the mission's 400th anniversary. It is a votive church dedicated to prayers that God would spare the world from atomic warfare.*

*The Shrine of Our Lady of la Leche is the first shrine dedicated to Our Blessed Mother in the United States. The devotion to Our Lady of la Leche was brought from Spain in 1598 by the Spanish settlers of St. Augustine. The present chapel dates from 1914 and is a replica of earlier coquina chapels. It houses a replica of the statue of Our Lady of la Leche and provides visitors with a quiet place to pray.*

*The Great Cross, made of stainless steel and rising 208 feet above the Matanzas marshes, stands as a sentinel over the Mission and a Beacon of Faith for all who pass by. It was erected at the direction of Archbishop Joseph P. Hurley and was dedicated during the diocesan Eucharistic Congress of October 1966. Like the Prince of Peace Church, the Great Cross celebrates the 400th anniversary of the founding of the Mission Nombre de De dios.*